T0151488

CLASSIC HOME COOKING FROM JAPAN

ASAKO YOSHIDA

TUTTLE Publishing

Tokyo | Rutland, Vermont | Singapore

Contents

Simmered Yellowtail and Daikon, *page 46*

Daikon Radish with Chicken-Miso Sauce, *page 58*

Temari Sushi Balls, *page 72*

Classic Japanese-style Home Cooking

Seasonal, Delicious and Flavorful

I decided to pursue a career promoting classic Japanese home cooking because I never get tired of eating it. I could be biased—it is, after all, the cuisine of my own country, but I hope that you, too, will never tire of the recipes in this book, wherever you're from.

I feel so grateful for my cooking heritage—whenever I deeply inhale the aroma of a traditional Japanese hot pot, whenever I make rice with green peas in the springtime, whenever I simmer root vegetables in the winter, or any time I can sense the changing of the seasons with my taste buds.

Classic Japanese cooking has four pillars:

Dashi stock

Dashi is the traditional stock used in Japanese cuisine, usually made from seaweed or fish. Instant dashi stock powder can be found in supermarkets worldwide, but for best results, try making your own dashi using one of the recipes on pages 6–7.

Seasonal food

The core concept of Japanese cooking is to eat foods that are in season. Seasonal ingredients are packed with aroma, umami, and inherently delicious flavors, as well as nutrition.

My goal with this book is to enable anyone in the world to cook all the classic recipes that Japanese people love to eat at home. I hope that you the reader can experience the joy and fun of cooking with your own hands as you develop your eye for selecting the right ingredients and the right cooking methods. Nothing would make me happier than for this book to become a part of your everyday life.

Asako Yoshida

Cooking with all five senses

Your hands are your best cooking tools—in other words, your sense of touch. In addition, use your eyes to observe, your ears to listen, and your sense of smell and taste to nail down the flavors of the food you are cooking.

Properly cooked rice

A Japanese meal is usually served with fluffy, warm, white rice. The medium-grain white rice used for the recipes in this book is best cooked in a rice cooker if you have one, or you can follow the instructions on page 80 to cook perfect rice in a regular pot.

How to Make Dashi Stock

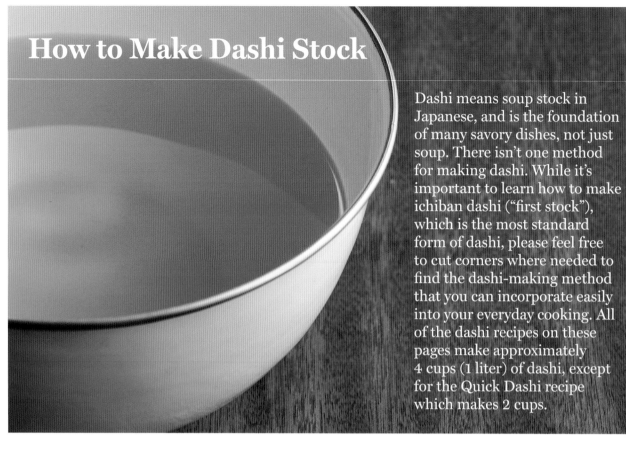

Dashi means soup stock in Japanese, and is the foundation of many savory dishes, not just soup. There isn't one method for making dashi. While it's important to learn how to make ichiban dashi ("first stock"), which is the most standard form of dashi, please feel free to cut corners where needed to find the dashi-making method that you can incorporate easily into your everyday cooking. All of the dashi recipes on these pages make approximately 4 cups (1 liter) of dashi, except for the Quick Dashi recipe which makes 2 cups.

Ichiban Dashi

1 piece dried kombu seaweed, about 4 x 2 in
   (10 x 5 cm)
4 cups (1 L) water
Handful dried bonito flakes, about ¼ oz (10 g)

1 Soak the kombu seaweed

Wipe the surface of the kombu with a moistened paper towel, and put in a pan with the 4 cups of water. Soak for at least 2 hours, or overnight.

2 Heat the water and take out the kombu seaweed

Heat the water over medium heat. Just before the water comes to a boil, take out the kombu.

3 Remove any scum

Remove any scum that comes to the surface. If you stop here, you have kombu dashi, which is called for in several recipes.

4 Add the bonito flakes

Sprinkle in the bonito flakes.

5 Bring to a boil, then leave to soak

Bring the water up to a boil and turn off the heat. Leave as is for about 3 minutes.

6 Strain

Line a strainer with a paper towel and place the strainer over a bowl. Pour in the dashi from step 5 to strain. If the dashi is not to be used right away, transfer to a container and refrigerate until ready to use.

Niban Dashi

Niban dashi means "second stock." Put the kombu seaweed and bonito flakes used to make ichiban dashi into a pan, and add 4 cups (1 L) of water. Heat over medium heat. When it comes to a boil, add a handful of bonito flakes (about ¼ oz/10 g). Simmer for 2 to 3 minutes and strain.

Water Dashi

Use the same amount of kombu seaweed, bonito flakes and water as for Ichiban Dashi. Put the bonito flakes into a straining bag, or a mesh strainer ball used for cooking herbs in soups. Quickly wipe the kombu seaweed with a moistened paper towel, and place both into a jar or pitcher. Add the water and refrigerate overnight.

Microwave Dashi

Use the same amount of kombu seaweed, bonito flakes and water as for Ichiban Dashi. Put the bonito flakes into a straining bag, or a mesh strainer ball used for cooking herbs in soups. Quickly wipe the kombu seaweed with a moistened paper towel, and cut or break into 3 or 4 pieces. Place both in a microwave-safe bowl and add the water. Microwave for about 6 minutes in a 600 watt microwave oven. Take out the kombu seaweed and straining bag or ball. Squeeze the bag into the bowl to extract all the liquid.

Quick Dashi

Makes about 2 cups (500 ml). Place a handful of bonito flakes (about ¼ oz/10 g) and a 4 in (10 cm) square piece of kombu seaweed that's been wiped quickly with a moistened paper towel, into a pan with 2 cups (500 ml) of water. Heat over medium heat. Just before it comes to a boil, remove the kombu seaweed. When the pan comes to a boil, turn off the heat and leave for about 3 minutes before straining.

Sardine Dashi

This uses dried sardines called niboshi, available at your Japanese grocery. Remove the heads and insides of a handful of niboshi (about ¼ oz/10 g) with your fingers. Put 4 cups (1 L) of water in a pan. Add a small piece of kombu that's been wiped with a moistened paper towel, and the niboshi. Soak for at least 2 hours or overnight. Bring the pan to a boil on medium heat. Turn off the heat, and leave for 3 minutes. Strain to remove the kombu and sardines.

Which dashi should I use?

Ichiban Dashi is the most fragrant and flavorful dashi and should be used in clear soups. For simmered dishes with lots of flavor, Niban Dashi is fine. Water Dashi is handy to have on hand. When you don't have time or when you just need a little dashi, use the Microwave Dashi or Quick Dashi recipes.

Ultimately the choice of base ingredients you use for your dashi depends on the ingredients you have available and on your personal preference.

All types of dashi will keep in the refrigerator for 4 to 5 days, or about a month in the freezer.

Glossary of Japanese Ingredients

Aburaage thin-fried tofu, sometimes called "fried-skin tofu" is a thin sheet of tofu that has been deep fried until golden brown. Available at Japanese grocery stores.

Beef *see* Thinly sliced meat

Bonito flakes are shaved from fermented, dried and aged skipjack tuna or bonito. They are an essential ingredient in Japanese cooking, used in dashi stock, and as a garnish. Flake size ranges from fine and powder-like to large, long shavings that look like wood shavings. Available at Japanese grocery stores or online.

Burdock root is a long, brown fibrous root vegetable with a wonderful aroma and crunchy texture. Available at Japanese, Korean and some general Asian stores.

Daikon radish is a thick white root vegetable. Spicy and crunchy when raw, it becomes soft and sweet when cooked. Find it at Asian grocery stores as well as at many regular supermarkets.

Kombu seaweed is a main ingredient in most types of dashi stock. It is sold in dried form and is available at Japanese grocery stores or online.

Kombu tea should not be confused with the fermented "mushroom" called kombucha which is an entirely different thing. Kombu tea is salted and dried kombu seaweed powder that is dissolved in hot water to make a quick, slightly salty beverage. It's used as a seasoning in cooking too. Available at Japanese grocery stores.

Konnyaku is a jelly-like food made from the corms of the konjac plant. It has little flavor, but easily absorbs any flavors it's cooked with. It's mainly enjoyed for its unique texture. It has almost no calories and lots of water-soluble fiber. It is sold in blocks packed in bags of water, and can be found at Japanese grocery stores or online.

Lotus Root is the rhizome of the lotus plant, with holes running through it that give an attractive, lacy appearance. You'll find it at most Asian grocery stores.

Mirin is a sweet, alcoholic liquor made from rice. Originally a drink, nowadays it's used almost exclusively for cooking. It is so sweet that it's often used instead of sugar in various recipes, and is a staple in any Japanese kitchen. Mirin is available at Japanese grocery stores or online.

Miso is a fermented paste made with soybeans plus wheat and/or rice. Two types are used in this book. Red miso is made mostly with soybeans, and is more strongly flavored and saltier than white miso (which is actually light brown). The latter is sweeter and contains more wheat.

Mitsuba (sometimes sold as Japanese parsley or honeywort) is a mild and fresh-tasting herb used as a garnish, available at well-stocked Japanese grocery stores and general Asian stores. If you can't find it, substitute mizuna greens, flat-leaf parsley or celery leaves, depending on the recipe.

Okara, translated as "soy pulp" or "tofu dregs" is the fibrous, insoluble parts of the soybean after the soy milk has been extracted. In Japan this is available very cheaply, but elsewhere it may be hard to find. If you have a tofu maker near you, ask them if they have okara. If you make your own soy milk or tofu, you will have plenty!

Ponzu sauce is made with a combination of citrus juice, vinegar, soy sauce, kombu seaweed and bonito flakes. It is salty, sour and packed with umami. You can substitute lemon or lime juice. Bottled ponzu sauce is available at Japanese grocery stores.

Pork *see* Thinly sliced meat

Rice. Medium-grain Japonica rice is recommended for the recipes in this book. It is sometimes sold as "sushi rice."

Sake is an alcoholic drink made from rice. It's used in cooking to add flavor and get rid of any "gaminess" in fish, poultry and meat. You can find cooking sake at Japanese groceries, or use regular drinking sake.

Sansho pepper is an aromatic spice with a citrusy tang and a tongue-numbing quality. The peppercorns are dried and ground into a powder or pickled. The fresh young leaves, called kinome, are used as a garnish.

Sesame oil. Two types are used in this book. Dark sesame oil is made with toasted sesame seeds, has an amber color, and a distinct sesame aroma. White sesame oil, made with raw sesame seeds, has a light aroma and color. The dark type is easy to find at Asian or Japanese grocery stores, but the light type may be difficult to source; you can use a light vegetable oil instead.

Shirataki noodles, made from konjac roots or glucomannan, have become very popular as a low-carb alternative to pasta. They are sometimes sold as "tofu shirataki."

Shiso leaves are widely used in Japanese cooking as a garnish, in salads and so on. Do not confuse shiso with *kkae* or Korean perilla, which looks similar but has an aniseed flavor and fragrance. Kkae has leaves with rounded points and purple-tinged undersides, while shiso leaves are lighter green, have spiky points and are often ruffled. You can find green shiso leaves at well-stocked Japanese grocery stores. It's also easy to grow from seed.

Soy sauce comes in different types, but most widely used in Japan is *koikuchi* or dark soy sauce. Another type of soy sauce that is becoming more available outside of Japan is *usukuchi* or light soy sauce. Although the name says "light", it is actuall higher in salt than dark soy sauce. Light so sauce is used in dishes where the flavor of soy sauce is required but not the dark color Unless specified, you can use either light or dark soy sauce in the recipes in this book.

Thinly sliced meat is used in many recipes in this book and can be found at Japanese, Korean and general Asian grocery stores. I you can't find pre-sliced meat, you can ask your butcher to slice a block of meat thinly for you. To slice your own, freeze the block of meat for about an hour to make it firm, which makes it easier to slice. Offcuts can be used in many recipes too. Beef meant for Philadelphia cheesesteak can also be used.

Umeboshi are salt-preserved ume plums, related to apricots but much tarter when ripe. They are usually quite salty and sour, although some types are sweetened with honey or sugar. Umeboshi (often abbreviated to *ume*) are used as a flavoring ingredient as well as eaten as-is.

Vinegar. This book uses rice vinegar or grain vinegar, made from rice or mixed grains. Both are mildly sour. Don't confuse rice vinegar with the product "sushi vinegar," which has added salt and sugar and is used to flavor sushi rice. This book also uses black vinegar (*kurosu*), which is rice vinegar mixed with rice koji (a type of mold) and aged. It has a mild sourness and rice flavor. Black vinegar is also used in Chinese food and can be found at Asian grocery stores.

Worcestershire sauce. The Japanese version is sweeter and thicker than its British equivalent. Chuunoh sauce is similar to Japanese-style Worcestershire sauce, as is tonkatsu sauce. Try substituting steak sauce for any of these, adding a little mirin, honey or sugar. The Japanese sauces are available at Japanese grocery stores.

Yuzu is a Japanese citrus, which you might find at your Japanese grocery store. If you can't find it, try lemon or lime instead.

CHAPTER 1

Ten Japanese Classics

To start things off, this chapter contains ten popular, traditional dishes that the Japanese eat at home. All you have to do is follow my simple step-by-step instructions, and you'll end up with the most delicious results!

Meat and Potato Hot Pot

Called *nikujaga* in Japan, this is the dish that most says "mom's cooking" to the Japanese. My recipe is designed to make sure the savory-sweet flavors permeate this homey, comforting dish, that is sure to become a favorite.

By pre-soaking the potatoes in water, parboiling the shirataki noodles, and prepping all the individual elements carefully before they come together, the final results will be that much tastier. I recommend that you don't stir-fry the beef beforehand, but simply simmer it instead, for more tender, juicy results.

Serves 2

–4 medium potatoes, peeled
medium onion
–8 fresh green beans
oz (125 g) shirataki noodles packed in
water, or dried bean thread noodles
tablespoon vegetable oil
oz (250 g) thinly sliced beef

For the simmering liquid
2 cups (500 ml) dashi stock
(see pages 6–7)
4 tablespoons mirin
4 tablespoons soy sauce
1½ tablespoons raw sugar

Note: Shirataki noodles, made from
konjac roots or glucomannan are
sometimes sold as "tofu shirataki." If
you can't find them, use dried bean
thread noodles instead.

1 Cut the ingredients

Cut the potatoes in half, then cut each
half into 2 or 3 pieces. Put the cut
potato pieces into a bowl of cold water,
and soak for about 10 minutes. This
will eliminate surface starch and give
the finished dish a clean taste. Cut the
onion into 8 wedges. Quickly cook the
green beans in boiling water, and cut
into 1¼ in (3 cm) long pieces.

2 Parboil the noodles

Shirataki noodles need to be
parboiled to remove any odor. Bring
a pan of water to a boil, put in the
noodles, and boil for 1 minute. Drain
into a colander. Cut the noodles into
2 to 3 pieces if they are long.

3 Stir-fry

Heat the vegetable oil in a pan over
medium heat. Add the potatoes and
onion, and stir-fry for a couple of
minutes until all the pieces are coated
with the oil.

**4 Add the simmering
liquid ingredients**

Combine the simmering liquid
ingredients in a bowl, and add to
the pan.

5 Add the noodles and beef

When the liquid comes to a boil, add
the shirataki or bean thread noodles
and the beef (cut into bite-size pieces
if needed) and mix quickly. When the
liquid comes back to a boil, turn the
heat down to low.

6 Simmer

Skim off any scum that rises to the
surface. Simmer until a bamboo
skewer goes easily through a piece of
potato. Arrange on a serving plate,
and scatter with the green beans.

Deep-fried Crunchy Chicken

This classic dish is called *karaage* in Japan. By following these three key points, your chicken is sure to turn out perfectly crisp and crunchy!

- The first key to success is to make sure the chicken is completely coated with the cornstarch mixture. Otherwise moisture will escape from any uncoated spots and the surface will not be properly crispy.

- The second key is to be patient and not move the chicken pieces around after you have put them into the hot oil. Wait until the surface has firmed up.

- The third key is to fry the chicken twice. After the first frying, rest the pieces. This will ensure a juicy result. Finish by frying again in very hot oil.

Serves 2

boneless chicken thighs,
about 8 oz (250 g) total
beaten egg
ornstarch, for coating
il, for deep-frying
ettuce leaves, to garnish
emon wedges, to garnish

For the marinade
1 tablespoon ginger juice
   (grate fresh ginger and squeeze
   it to extract the juice)
1½ tablespoons soy sauce
1½ tablespoons sake
Black pepper, to taste

1 Prepare the chicken

Remove any excess fat (mainly the
ellow parts), the edges of the skin
hat go beyond the meat, any hard
parts or sinew. (I recommend working
ith a small knife.) Cut into large
ite-size pieces, since the meat will
hrink when it's cooked.

2 Marinate the chicken

Combine the marinade ingredients
in a bowl, add the chicken from
Step 1 and squeeze it around in the
marinade with your hands. Leave for
about 15 minutes.

3 Add the egg

Drain the marinade from the chicken.
Add the beaten egg and rub it in well,
using your hands.

4 Coat with the cornstarch

Pat the marinated and egged chicken
ightly with paper towels. Coat
ompletely and evenly with the
cornstarch.

5 Deep-fry

Put the oil in a pan or frying pan,
and heat it to 340°F (170°C). Add
the coated chicken from Step 4, and
do not move around until the surface
has firmed up. When the surface is
firm, turn occasionally and fry until
the pieces are a light golden brown.
Take the chicken pieces out of the oil
and rest for 4 to 5 minutes.

6 Rest and deep-fry again

Heat the oil to 355°F (180°C). Add the
rested chicken pieces from Step 5 and
fry until crispy on the surface. Drain
off the oil and arrange on a plate with
lettuce leaves and lemon wedges.

Pan-fried Pork with Ginger

With the spicy zing of ginger and a savory-sweet sauce, ginger pork is a perfect accompaniment to plain steamed rice.

The key to this dish is to sever the sinews of the pork beforehand, to prevent it from shrinking and turning tough when it's cooked. The meat is then sautéed quickly over high heat so that it doesn't overcook. The result is a nutty, flavorful surface and meat that's tender and juicy when you bite into it.

Serves 2

–8 slices boneless pork loin, ¼ in (6 mm)
thick, about 8 oz (250g) total
teaspoons dark sesame oil

For the marinade
1 tablespoon ginger juice (grate fresh
    ginger and squeeze to extract the juice)
2 tablespoons soy sauce
2 tablespoons sake
2 tablespoons mirin

Garnishes
Finely shredded cabbage
Thinly sliced red onion

1 Cut the pork sinews

Make 3 small cuts on the border of
the meat and the fat, to prevent the
meat from curling when cooked. You
only need to do this on one side.

2 Marinate

Combine the marinade ingredients
in a bowl, and pour into a shallow
tray. Put the prepped pork from Step
1 into the tray in a single layer, and
turn once.

3 Leave for 5 minutes

Leave the pork to marinate for about
5 minutes. Do not marinate for too
long or the meat will become tough.

4 Pan-fry the pork

Heat the sesame oil in a frying pan.
Remove the pork from the marinade
(reserving the marinade) and fry in a
frying pan over medium-high heat in
a single layer. Quickly fry both sides.

5 Add the marinade

Pour the reserved marinade into the
frying pan, and turn the pork several
times to coat it with the sauce on
both sides. Arrange on serving plates
with shredded cabbage and sliced
onion on the side.

Mackerel in Miso Sauce

Although simmered dishes have a reputation for taking a long time to make, fish only takes a short time to cook through, so simmered fish dishes like this one don't take long.

Oily blue fish like mackerel need to be pre-treated by pouring boiling water over them quickly (this is called "frosting" in Japanese since the surface turns white). This is an extra step, but by doing this you barely need to remove any scum from the surface of the cooking liquid as the fish simmers, and any fishy odor will also be eliminated.

Serves 4

old water, for rinsing
 pieces fresh mackerel,
 4–5 oz (100–125 g) each
oiling water, for pre-treating
 cup (160 ml) water

⅔ cup (160 ml) sake
4 thin slices ginger
3 tablespoons red miso
1½ tablespoons white miso
1 tablespoon raw sugar

Garnishes
1 piece ginger, peeled and finely
   shredded
Green part of 2–3 green onions
   (scallions), sliced thinly diagonally

1 Pour on boiling water on the mackerel

repare a bowl of cold water ready
r Step 2. Make a crisscross cut into
ach mackerel piece. Place in a large
olander or on a large sieve, and pour
oiling water over them. Turn the
ackerel and pour boiling water over
e other side. Make sure you don't
iss any spots with the boiling water.

2 Wipe the mackerel

Immediately plunge the mackerel in
the bowl of cold water. Rinse quickly,
and wipe with paper towels to remove
any surface sliminess or blood.

3 Start heating

Put the cleaned mackerel pieces in
a pan and add the ⅔ cup of water,
the sake and the ginger slices. Mix
quickly, then turn the heat to high.

4 Simmer

hen the liquid comes to a boil, turn
e heat to medium low and skim off
ny scum. Place a small lid directly
n top of the contents of the pan (this
 called a drop lid, see page 80), or
se a piece of kitchen parchment
aper with a slit cut in the middle.
immer for about 10 minutes until
e mackerel is cooked through.

5 Add the miso

Put the red miso and white miso
in a small bowl, add a little of the
cooking liquid, and mix to form a
smooth paste. Add this paste with
the sugar to the pan, put the drop
lid or kitchen parchment paper back
on, and simmer for about 5 minutes
until the sauce has thickened slightly.
Transfer to serving plates and serve
with the shredded ginger and thinly
sliced green onion on top.

Potato Croquettes

Creamy on the inside, crispy on the outside, with the sweetness of onions and the umami of ground meat, these traditional Japanese-style potato croquettes are sure to become a favorite!

The most important point is to boil the potatoes in their skins to ensure they stay fluffy. Chop the onions very finely, and sauté them well to draw out their sweetness. Make sure the onions and ground meat are evenly distributed in the mashed potato.

Makes 8

medium potatoes
2 tablespoon olive oil
2 medium onion, finely chopped
oz (100 g) ground beef
little salt and pepper
little ground nutmeg
flour, for dusting
beaten egg
breadcrumbs, for coating
oil, for deep-frying

For the sauce
1 tablespoon ketchup
1 tablespoon Japanese-style
    Worcestershire sauce
1 tablespoon Chuunoh sauce, or
    steak sauce

Garnishes
Shredded lettuce
Cherry tomatoes

Note: Japanese-style Worcestershire sauce and Chuunoh are very similar to each other, but Chuunoh sauce is a bit thicker and sweeter. Both are available at Japanese grocery stores. You can try steak sauce instead. Potato croquettes are also delicious without any sauce.

1 Boil the potatoes

Wash the potatoes but don't peel them. Cut them into a pot with plenty of cold water over high heat. When the water comes to a boil, turn the heat to low and simmer the potatoes for 15 to 20 minutes until a wooden skewer goes through them easily. Drain.

2 Peel and mash the potatoes

Peel the potatoes while they are still hot using a fork or a skewer (protect your hands by holding the potatoes with a kitchen towel). Put the peeled potatoes in a bowl and mash.

3 Sauté the ground beef

Heat the olive oil in a frying pan over medium heat. Add the onion and sauté until transparent and lightly browned. Add the ground beef, and sauté until it changes color. Add the salt, pepper and nutmeg, and mix.

4 Form the patties

Add the cooked ground beef to the mashed potatoes and mix well. Divide into 8 portions, and form each into an oval patty.

5 Bread the patties

Coat the patties with flour, beaten egg and breadcrumbs, in that order. Make sure to coat each patty completely and evenly with a light coating of flour, gently shaking off any excess.

6 Deep-fry

Put the frying oil into a pot or deep frying pan and heat to 340°F (170°C), then add the breaded croquettes. Do not try to move them around until the surface has firmed up. Turn when one side is a light golden brown, then turn the heat up. Turn the croquettes several times until they are browned and crispy. Drain off the oil and serve with the lettuce and cherry tomatoes. Combine the sauce ingredients and serve on the side—each diner can put on as much as they like.

Japanese Rolled Omelet

This classic egg dish, called *tamagoyaki* in Japanese, is made using a square tamagoyaki pan, which you can find at Japanese kitchen-supply stores or online. The omelet has a reputation for being hard to make, but it's actually easy to master with a little practice and by paying attention to the key points below.

- Don't worry if the first one or two layers are too thin or fall apart a bit.

- If you think the egg is cooking too fast, take it off the heat and take a little break.

- Try lifting up the far end of the tamagoyaki pan and shaking the pan while rolling the egg.

- If your final egg roll is a bit ragged, you can tidy it up by wrapping it in a sushi mat.

Makes 1 roll

3 large eggs

4 tablespoons dashi stock (see pages 6–7)

½ teaspoon light soy sauce

Oil, for cooking

A little grated daikon radish, for garnish

Note: For this recipe, you will need a square or rectangular tamagoyaki pan. The best tamagoyaki pans are made of copper, but are pricey. A second best choice is an aluminum one with a non-stick coating. If you can master using cooking chopsticks you'll find that helpful for this recipe. A sushi rolling mat is also useful. All 3 items are available at Japanese grocery stores or online.

① Beat the egg, add the stock

Break the eggs into a bowl and beat with a fork or cooking chopsticks. If using chopsticks, keep the points in contact with the bottom of the bowl at all times and quickly move them from left to right. This way the egg will not get foamy (which leads to bubbles forming in the omelet) and the egg white will break apart better. Add the dashi and soy sauce, and mix quickly.

② Strain the egg

Strain the egg mixture through a fine mesh sieve.

③ Transfer to the pan

Heat a tamagoyaki pan over medium heat. Soak a wadded up piece of paper towel in oil, and spread a generous amount of oil around the bottom and sides of the pan. When the pan has heated up, pour about a quarter of the egg mixture into the pan and cook.

④ Roll the egg

When the edges of the egg in the pan start to firm up, burst any bubbles that have formed with your fork or chopsticks, and roll the egg from the far side towards you (or vice versa, whichever is easier for you) using a spatula or chopsticks.

⑤ Pour and roll again

Push the rolled up egg to the far side of the pan. Spread a generous amount of oil in the pan again using the wadded up paper towel, then add another quarter of the egg liquid to the pan. Immediately lift up the rolled cooked egg so that the egg liquid can flow below it (see photo). Roll the egg in the same way as in Step 4. Repeat these steps twice more until all the egg liquid has been used up.

⑥ Roll the egg in a sushi mat

Put the cooked rolled egg onto a sushi mat. Roll the sushi mat around the egg and squeeze gently to tidy up the shape of the roll. Let the roll rest in the sushi mat for 3 to 4 minutes, unroll, and slice the egg into thick pieces. Garnish with grated daikon radish on the side, if you like.

Sweet and Savory Pork Belly

In this recipe, pork belly is simmered gently until it falls apart under your fork. My cooking method ensures that the pork becomes tender without getting greasy—just let the pork cool down completely in its cooking liquid before serving so that any excess fat that gathers on the surface can be removed easily. That way you'll have a melt-in-your-mouth dish that will have your family clamoring for more!

Serves 2

 oz (400 g) pork belly block
reen part of 1 baby leek or 2
fat green onions
 slices unpeeled ginger
½ cups (625 ml) water
 blanched bok choy leaves,
for garnish

The flavorings
4 tablespoons soy sauce
½ cup (125 ml) sake
2 tablespoons raw sugar

1 **Cut the pork**

ut the pork belly into 1½ in (4 cm)
ubes.

2 **Brown the pork**

Heat a frying pan (preferably a cast-iron one), put in the pork, and brown over medium-high heat while turning frequently. Wipe out the fat that is exuded from the meat with wadded up paper towels.

3 **Simmer**

Put the browned pork, leek or green onion, ginger and water in a pan. Bring to a boil, skim off any scum, turn the heat down to low and simmer for about 90 minutes.

4 **Add the flavorings**

dd the flavorings to the pan and
immer for another 30 minutes.
urn off the heat and cool for a while,
nen transfer to a storage container
nd refrigerate for at least 2 hours or
vernight.

5 **Remove the fat**

Remove any hardened fat from the surface. Return the pork and liquid to a pan and heat through before serving. Serve with pieces of blanched bok choy on the side. (See page 28 for how to blanch.)

Crispy Fried Mackerel

This mouthwatering dish is a Japanese standard, and the perfect accompaniment to plain rice and miso soup. It's great simply served with a sprinkle of salt, but here I have served a slightly sweet tartar sauce on the side.

Traditionally this recipe uses butterflied fish. You can butterfly the fish yourself following my step-by-step instructions, or ask a fishmonger to do this for you. You may be able to find horse mackerel that's been butterflied for making this dish at well-stocked Japanese grocery stores.

Serves 2

4 small horse mackerel, or
 other small, whole oily fish,
 about 3 oz (75 g) each
Salt and pepper, to taste
Flour, for coating
Beaten egg, for coating
Breadcrumbs, for coating
Oil, for deep-frying

For the tartar sauce
1 hard-boiled egg
4 green shiso or basil leaves
6 small pickled onions
1 teaspoon pickling liquid
2 tablespoons mayonnaise

Garnishes
Shredded cabbage
Parsley

Note: If you can't find mackerel, this cooking method can be used for any similar small oily fish. Thin fillets may also be used, like sardines.

1 Prep the fish

Cut off the bony strips on both sides of the fish and remove the scales. Cut off the heads, remove the intestines and rinse under running water. Pat dry.

2 Butterfly the fish

Insert your knife into the back of the fish towards the spine. Push the knife between the flesh and the bone, and slowly open up the fish while moving the knife, taking care not to cut through the skin of the belly. Repeat on the other side of the fish. Chop off the spine, leaving the tail attached, and remove any small bones that may remain.

3 Add salt and pepper

Put the butterflied fish in a single layer in a shallow tray with the skin sides down. Salt and pepper the fish on the side facing up only.

4 Bread the fish

Coat the fish with flour, beaten egg and breadcrumbs, in that order. Make sure to coat each fish completely and evenly with a light coating of flour, brushing off any excess.

5 Deep-fry

Put the oil into a pot or deep frying pan and heat to 340°F (170°C), then put in the breaded fish. Do not try to move them around until the surface has firmed up. Turn once one side is a light golden brown, then turn the heat up. Turn the fish several times until they are browned and crispy. Drain off the oil.

6 Make the tartar sauce

Finely chop the hard-boiled egg. Chop up the shiso leaves and pickled onions roughly. Put all three in a bowl, add the rest of the tartar sauce ingredients and mix well. Arrange the fried fish on plates with shredded cabbage, parsley and the tartar sauce on the side.

Braised Chicken and Vegetables

The rich flavor of this dish is achieved by stir-frying the ingredients in sesame oil. You can make this a vegan dish by omitting the chicken—the results will still taste great.

Serves 2

5 oz (125 g) boneless chicken thigh meat
½ tablespoon sake
⅓ burdock root (optional)
½ carrot, peeled
2 in (5 cm) piece lotus root, peeled
2 dried shiitake mushrooms
6–8 snow peas
1 piece konnyaku (optional),
  about 3 oz (75 g)
½ tablespoon dark sesame oil

For the braising liquid
1¾ cups (425 ml) dashi stock
  (see pages 6–7)
2 tablespoons sake
1 tablespoon raw sugar
1 tablespoon mirin
2 tablespoons soy sauce

The key is to stir-fry everything well so that all the ingredients are coated with the oil, and the vegetables are shiny.

1 **Chop and prep the ingredients**

Remove excess fat or sinew from the chicken, cut into bite-size pieces and sprinkle with the sake. Shave the burdock root, if using, following the instructions on page 28, then roughly chop. Roughly chop the carrot and lotus root. Put the burdock root and lotus root in two separate bowls of cold water for a few minutes, then drain in a colander. Soak the dried shiitake for 20 minutes in hot water to rehydrate them, cut off and discard the stems and cut the caps into quarters. Remove the strings from the snow peas and blanch in boiling water (see page 28 for how to blanch). Take out the snow peas. If using konnyaku, cut into bite-size pieces and boil for 2 to 3 minutes in the same water.

2 **Stir-fry**

Heat the sesame oil in a pan over medium heat, add the chicken and stir-fry briefly. When the chicken changes color, add the burdock root, carrot, shiitake and konnyaku. Stir-fry until everything is well coated with the oil.

3 **Simmer**

Add all the braising liquid ingredients except the soy sauce and turn the heat to high. When the liquid comes to a boil skim off any scum, and cover with a small lid that fits inside the pan or place a piece of kitchen parchment paper with several holes in it right on top of the contents of the pan. Simmer for about 12 minutes over low heat.

4 **Add the soy sauce**

Add the soy sauce, and simmer for another 8 minutes while occasionally mixing the contents of the pan from the bottom up. Serve with the snow peas on top.

Winter Hot Pot

This traditional winter hot pot is called *oden* in Japan. If you live near a well-stocked Japanese supermarket, have a go at using some of the more unfamiliar ingredients—they may become favorites! Or simply use the broth to make a warming hot pot with other ingredients of your choice.

Serves 2

- oz (175 g) daikon radish
- piece konnyaku (optional), about 6 oz (175 g)
- boneless chicken thigh, about 4 oz (100 g)
- boiled baby octopus legs, about 4 oz (100 g)
- hard-boiled eggs
- fried fish cake stuffed with burdock root (gobo-ten), or other Asian fish cake
- blocks thick, fried tofu (atsuage) cut in half or quarters

For the broth
- ½ cups (625 ml) dashi stock, (see pages 6–7)
- tablespoons sake
- tablespoons mirin
- ½ tablespoons light soy sauce
- tablespoon dark soy sauce
- ¼ teaspoon salt

Since there are many ingredients in this hot pot, add the ones that take longer to cook first, and add the ones that take less time later.

Note: The boiled octopus legs, gobo-ten and atsuage are available in the refrigerated section of Japanese grocery stores. The octopus legs may be found in the sashimi section. You can also use other types of fried tofu, pressed tofu, Asian fish cakes, squid and root vegetables that are available in your local supermarket. The important thing is the broth!

1 Parboil the daikon and konnyaku

Peel and cut the daikon radish into ¾ in (2 cm) thick slices. Put into a pot with cold water, bring to a boil and simmer for 20 minutes until tender. If using konnyaku, cut it into triangles, put into a pan of boiling water, boil for about 3 minutes then drain.

2 Begin with ingredients that take longest

Put the broth ingredients in a pot (an earthenware one is ideal, but any heavy pot will do) over medium heat. Remove any excess fat or sinew from the chicken thigh, cut into bite-size pieces and add to the pot once the soup has come to a boil. Simmer until it is cooked through. Add the daikon radish, konnyaku and octopus, and simmer over low heat for about 1 hour.

3 Add the other ingredients

Cut up the gobo-ten and add to the soup with the boiled eggs and atsuage. Simmer over low heat for another 30 minutes.

4 Cool down

Turn the heat off and let the pot cool down while the ingredients absorb the flavors of the soup. Heat up just before serving.

Measuring, Cutting and Prepping

How to Measure Powders and Liquids

When using a measuring spoon, use the handle of another spoon or a similar implement to level out the ingredient in the spoon.

1 teaspoon

½ teaspoon

⅔ teaspoon

A little salt

The amount of salt you can hold between your thumb and forefinger.

A pinch of salt

The amount of salt you can hold between your thumb, forefinger and middle finger.

Measuring cups

When measuring ingredients in cups, check the amount with the cup held up to your line of sight.

How to Cut Vegetables

Roughly cut eggplants
Cut the off the calyx, and slice the eggplant diagonally. Rotate the eggplant as you continue to cut so the pieces are roughly triangular. This maximizes the cut surface of the eggplant.

How to shave burdock
Wash the burdock root, and make a deep crisscross cut in one end. Working over a bowl filled with water, shave thin strips off it (as if you are sharpening a pencil) while turning the burdock root from time to time.

Finely chopped onion

1. Halve the onion. Leaving the part around the root end intact, make several thin cuts going with the grain.
2. Hold your knife parallel to the cutting board, and make 3–4 horizontal cuts.
3. Chop vertically from the end opposite the root. Discard the hard root.
4. Chop to even up the size of the pieces.

rounds

half rounds

quarters

matchsticks

strips

julienned

thin diagonal slices

diced

How to Prepare Other Vegetables

Rubbing with salt
Put the cut-up vegetable in a bowl and add salt (for one small cucumber, add about 2 pinches). Rub and squeeze in the salt, mix, and leave for 5–10 minutes. Squeeze out the excess moisture.

Rolling on a board
Put the vegetables on a cutting board, sprinkle with salt and roll the vegetables firmly on the board. For okra, cut off the calyx after rolling, and peel any tough bits left.

Blanching
Bring a pan of water to a boil and add 2 pinches of salt. Add the vegetables, and boil until bright green and plump. Drain into a sieve or colander, and leave to cool.

CHAPTER 2
Meat and Fish Main Dishes

In this chapter you'll learn how to prepare and cook a range of flavorful meat and fish main dishes that all go really well with rice.

Tonkatsu Pork Cutlet

Tonkatsu is a breaded, deep-fried pork cutlet. Use fresh breadcrumbs, for a light, crispy finish and juicy meat. Another key is to coat the pork with breadcrumbs twice. This way the coating won't come off easily in the oil, which makes frying the cutlets foolproof!

Make several vertical cuts through the fat and the lean part of the meat, to prevent the cutlet from deforming.

Coat the pork with breadcrumbs and dip in beaten egg.

Serves 2

2 thick pieces pork loin, about 12–16 oz (350–450 g) total
Flour, for coating
Beaten egg, for coating
Breadcrumbs, for coating (see Note)
Oil, for deep-frying
Tonkatsu sauce, Japanese Worcestershire sauce or steak sauce
Shredded cabbage, for garnish
Radish sprouts, for garnish

Note: Panko Japanese-style breadcrumbs are now widely available. You can make your own breadcrumbs by whirring day old sliced bread in a food processor or blender. Stop when the crumbs are still quite rough. Alternatively, grate bread that has been in the freezer for half an hour using a cheese grater.

1. Make several cuts along the dividing line between the fat and the lean meat, to prevent the meat from shrinking when it is fried.

2. Lightly coat the pork slices on both sides with flour, and shake off any excess.

3. Dip the floured pork in beaten egg, then coat with the breadcrumbs, pressing them lightly onto the surface of the pork.

4. Dip the breaded pork in beaten egg again, and coat with more breadcrumbs.

5. Put the oil into a pot or deep frying pan and heat to 350°F (175°C). Put in the breaded pork. When the breading on one side has firmed up, turn the pork. Deep-fry until the pork is crispy and golden brown on both sides.

6. Drain the oil from the pork well. Slice into easy-to-eat pieces, and serve with cabbage and radish sprouts on the side.

VARIATION

Mini Pork Cutlets with Plum Miso

Bite-size cutlets are flavored with umeboshi plum.

Serves 2

10 pieces thinly sliced pork loin, about 4 oz (100 g) total
Flour, for coating
Beaten egg, for coating
Fresh breadcrumbs, for coating
Oil, for deep-frying
Radish sprouts, for garnish

For the plum miso
1 umeboshi pickled plum
1 tablespoon miso paste
2 teaspoons mirin

1. Remove the pit from the umeboshi pickled plum and chop the flesh into a paste. Combine with the other plum-miso ingredients in a bowl.

2. Spread out the pork slices and spread thinly with the plum miso. Roll up the pork to form triangular parcels.

3. Coat the rolled-up pork in flour, beaten egg and breadcrumbs, in that order. Deep-fry in 350°F (175°C) oil until golden brown and crispy. Drain off the oil, and serve the mini cutlets with radish sprouts on the side.

The plum-miso paste is salty so spread it very thinly (photo a). Roll up the pork slices diagonally so that they form triangular parcels (photo b), then add the breading.

Chicken Teriyaki

Teriyaki is probably one of the most famous Japanese cooking styles in the world, and it can be used for meat, poultry, fish or vegetables. Teriyaki sauce is easy to make, with just soy sauce, sake and mirin in equal amounts, plus a little sugar to taste.

read out the chicken, and make several all cuts in the meat so that it cooks more enly.

the skin side until very crispy; this way e meat side will gradually cook through too d turn out very juicy. To prevent the chicken m becoming greasy, carefully remove any cess fat from the pan with a paper towel.

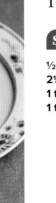

Serves 2

2 boneless chicken thighs with skin on, about 8 oz (250 g)
½ tablespoon vegetable oil

For the teriyaki sauce
1½ tablespoons soy sauce
1½ tablespoons sake
1½ tablespoons mirin
2 teaspoons raw sugar

Garnish
Blanched broccoli florets

1 Remove any excess fat and sinew from the chicken. Make horizontal cuts in the thick parts of the meat and spread them out, so that the meat is uniform in thickness. Make several small cuts in the meat.

2 Heat the vegetable oil in a frying pan, and put in the prepped chicken skin-side down. Fry over medium heat, wiping out any fat that comes out of the chicken with a wadded-up paper towel.

3 When the skin is well browned, turn the chicken over and cook for an additional 4 minutes.

4 Combine the teriyaki sauce ingredients and put in the pan with the chicken. Coat the chicken with the sauce while turning it frequently, until the surface is shiny and the sauce has thickened. Turn off the heat.

5 Slice the chicken into easy-to-eat pieces, and arrange on a plate with some broccoli florets that have been boiled briefly in salted water.

The essence of teriyaki is the *teri*, which means "shine" in Japanese. Coat the chicken well with the sauce. Cook over medium-high heat until it the sauce has thickened and the moisture has almost gone. If the frying pan is too big the sauce won't coat the chicken very well, so use one that matches the size of the chicken.

VARIATION

Curried Chicken Teriyaki

The curry flavor adds a twist to this classic dish.

Serves 2

½ tablespoon sake
2½ tablespoons mirin
1 tablespoon soy sauce
1 teaspoon curry powder

Follow Steps 1 to 3 of the Chicken Teriyaki recipe (above). Combine the sauce ingredients listed here and continue with the rest of the recipe.

Hamburger Steaks with Tofu

Hamburger steaks that contain tofu, which are lower fat than all-meat hamburger steaks, make frequent appearances at dinner in my house. I serve them with grated daikon radish and ponzu sauce. Since the flavors are quite simple, I add some texture with lotus root.

...sing a mixture of grated and chopped ...tus root creates different textures and ...dds crunch. It also makes the patties ...ght and airy.

When mixing all the ingredients in Step 2, make sure that no lumps of tofu remain. Mix well until the texture is smooth.

Serves 2

½ block firm tofu, about 4 oz (100 g)
1 lotus root, about 4 oz (100 g), peeled
5 oz (125 g) ground beef
5 oz (125 g) ground pork
1 beaten egg
A little salt
1 tablespoon cornstarch
1 teaspoon vegetable oil
A little sake

Garnishes
10–12 sugar snap peas
Grated daikon radish
Ponzu sauce

Note: In Japan it is common to mix beef and pork for this recipe, but it is fine to use just one type.

...nce both sides of the patties are browned, ... over the pan with a lid to steam-fry them ...oroughly. Steam-frying is an effective ...ethod for foods that don't cook through ...asily.

1. Drain the excess water from the tofu (see page 80). Grate half the lotus root, and cut the rest into ¼ in (6 mm) dice. Boil the sugar snap peas briefly in salted water.

2. Put the beef and pork into a bowl, and add the lotus root, tofu, beaten egg, salt and cornstarch. Mix well until the meat is sticky. Divide the mixture into 2, and form each portion into an oval patty. Make a dent in the middle of each patty.

3. Heat the vegetable oil in a frying pan, put in the patties and fry over medium heat. When the bottom side is browned, turn the patties over. Sprinkle in a little sake, turn the heat to low, put on a lid and steam-fry for 2 to 3 minutes.

4. Arrange on serving plates with the sugar snap peas on the side. Top with grated daikon radish and pour on some ponzu sauce before eating.

VARIATION

Meatballs with Sweet & Sour Sauce

Use the same meat mixture but change up the flavors completely!

Serves 2

For the meatballs
The same ingredients as the hamburger steaks
Oil, for deep-frying

For the sauce
1 tablespoon soy sauce
1 tablespoon sake
3 tablespoon rice vinegar
3 tablespoons sugar
1 teaspoon cornstarch
1 teaspoon water

1. Follow Steps 1 and 2 of the Hamburger Steaks recipe (above). Form the mixture into bite-size meatballs.

2. Heat some oil in a deep frying pan to 340°F (170°C). Put in the meatballs, and fry until brown while rolling them around. Drain off the oil.

3. Put the sauce ingredients into another frying pan, and bring to a boil while stirring. When the sauce has thickened, add the meatballs and toss to coat.

Tender Pork with Sesame Sauce

This tender, juicy pork dish is easy to make even if you've never tried cooking a block of meat. It's also very versatile—try serving the pork with different sauces or shredding any leftovers to use in stir-fries. It can also be served in the cooking liquid, which makes a delicious soup.

is photo shows the pork after salting and sting for 30 minutes. Pat the meat dry terwards, to eliminate the moisture that ntains much of the gamy flavor of the meat. e cooking liquid will remain clear and atively free of scum. If you have time, rest e pork overnight or even for a few days in the frigerator to age it and deepen the flavor.

n't eat the pork as soon as it's cooked; ave it to cool in the cooking liquid. Also ore leftover pork immersed in the cooking uid if possible. This will keep the meat juicy.

Serves 2

1 teaspoon salt
Block of pork shoulder, about 14 oz (400 g)
1 celery stalk, including the leaves
Green part of 1 baby leek or of 2 fat green onions
2–3 slices ginger, unpeeled
1 in (2.5 cm) square piece dried kombu seaweed
5 cups (1.25 L) water

Garnishes

1 small Japanese or Chinese eggplant
1 baby leek or 2 fat green onions
10 green shiso or basil leaves
1 large piece young ginger, or 2 myoga ginger buds

For the sauce

1 tablespoon soy sauce
1 tablespoon rice vinegar
White sesame seeds
Chili pepper powder, to taste

1. Rub the salt into the pork, and rest for at least 30 minutes. Pat dry with paper towels.

2. Put the pork, celery, leek or green onions, ginger, kombu seaweed and water into a pot over medium heat. Bring to a boil, take out the kombu seaweed, and simmer for about 20 minutes while skimming off any scum. Turn off the heat and leave to cool.

3. Prepare the garnishes. Grill the eggplant until charred all over, peel off the skin and shred into strips. Slice the baby leek into thin diagonal slices. Shred the shiso or basil leaves and ginger.

4. Combine the sauce ingredients. Remove the pork from the cooking liquid (you can reserve the liquid for another use, such as Pork Soup with Noodles, below). Arrange slices of pork on a plate with the eggplant, baby leek and ginger on the side. Dress with the sauce before eating.

VARIATION

Pork Soup with Noodles

Don't throw away the cooking liquid from Tender Pork with Sesame Sauce, use it for this dish!

Serves 2

2 slices boiled pork
½ green onion (scallion)
2 portions dried udon noodles

1¾ cups (425 ml) pork cooking liquid (left over from the Tender Pork with Sesame Sauce recipe, above)
Salt and pepper, to taste

1. Cut the pork into thin strips. Slice the onion in rounds.

2. Bring plenty of water to a boil in a pot, and cook the udon noodles, following the instructions on the packet. Drain.

3. Bring the pork cooking liquid to a boil in another pan. Taste, and season if needed with salt and pepper.

4. Put the cooked noodles in serving bowls and add the soup. Top with the pork and green onion.

Beef and Asparagus Rolls

By wrapping asparagus with thinly sliced beef and pan-frying the rolls quickly, you have a great main dish that is perfect to eat with rice. I've kept the seasoning simple too, just using soy sauce You can use other vegetables, or pork instead of beef.

Serves 2

4 large asparagus stalks
4 large thin slices beef, about 6 oz (175 g) total
Salt and pepper, to taste
2 teaspoons vegetable oil
1 tablespoon dark soy sauce

1 Remove the tough outer skin of the root end of the asparagus stalks using a vegetable peeler.

2 Spread out the beef slices and sprinkle with salt and pepper. Place an asparagus stalk on a slice of beef at the end closest to you, and roll the beef around the asparagus. Repeat for all the beef and asparagus.

3 Heat the oil in a frying pan. Put in the beef and asparagus rolls with the seam sides down, and fry over medium heat. Once the seam sides are stuck together, roll the rolls around in the frying pan to cook them evenly.

4 Add the dark soy sauce to the pan and move the rolls around to coat them. Cut the rolls in half and serve.

Stuffed Bell Peppers

The slightly sweet ketchup-based sauce used for these stuffed peppers makes me feel nostalgic for my childhood. Dusting the peppers with flour beforehand is the secret to keeping the stuffing intact as the peppers cook.

Serves 2

4 small bell peppers or padrone
  peppers (see Note)
1 tablespoon breadcrumbs
1½ tablespoons milk
Flour, for dusting
2 teaspoons vegetable oil
2 tablespoons white wine
2 tablespoons ketchup

For the filling
8 oz (225 g) ground pork
¼ medium onion, finely chopped
½ medium carrot, finely chopped
Salt and pepper, to taste

Note: Japanese green bell peppers are quite small, about the size of padrone peppers. Increase the amount of stuffing if using larger bell peppers.

1 Cut the bell peppers in half lengthwise, and remove the seeds, calyxes and white parts inside. Put the breadcrumbs and milk in a small bowl and leave until the breadcrumbs are moist.

2 In a separate large bowl, add the moistened breadcrumbs and the filling ingredients, and mix thoroughly with your hands.

3 Lightly dust the insides of the bell peppers with flour using a small sieve. Divide the meat mixture into 8 portions, and stuff the peppers so that the filling is nicely mounded.

5 Heat the oil in a frying pan, and put in the peppers with the meat filling side facing down. Fry over medium heat until the meat is browned. Turn the heat to low, cover the pan with a lid and steam-fry for 5 to 6 minutes. When the peppers are cooked through, remove from the frying pan to a serving plate.

6 Put the wine in the same frying pan, turn the heat to medium, and use a spatula to stir the wine while scraping the pan. Add the ketchup and stir until the sauce has thickened. Pour the sauce over the peppers.

Chicken Wings in Black Vinegar Sauce

Mildly sour and full of flavor, black vinegar makes this dish taste very refined even though it's so easy. Black vinegar is used in China as well as Japan, and is available at Asian grocery stores.

By blanching the chicken before cooking, the particular odor it has (which is considered undesirable in Japanese cooking), as well as any extra fat, will be eliminated. You just need to boil it for about 20 seconds, until the surface of the chicken has tightened up.

Serves 2

4 whole chicken wings
2 hard-boiled eggs, peeled

For the simmering sauce
2 slices ginger
¾ cup (185 ml) dashi stock (see pages 6–7)
2½ tablespoons soy sauce
½ cup (125 ml) sake
½ cup (125 ml) black vinegar

1 Bring some water to a boil in a pan and blanch the chicken wings (see photo caption for how to blanch). Drain in a colander.

2 Put all the simmering sauce ingredients in a pan and bring to a boil over medium heat. Add the blanched chicken wings and the hard-boiled eggs. Cover with a small lid that sits right on top of the ingredients in the pan, or a piece of kitchen parchment paper with several holes cut into it, and simmer over low heat for about 20 minutes, or until the liquid has reduced to a third of its original volume. Check regularly to skim off any scum. Cut the boiled eggs in half lengthwise, and serve the eggs, chicken wings and sauce in bowls.

VARIATION

Fragrant Chicken Rice

Mix the flavor-packed chicken-wing meat with fragrant herbs in rice

Serves 2

2 Chicken Wings in Black
    Vinegar Sauce (see above)
½ bunch mitsuba, or other
    greens (see Note)
1½ tablespoons gari pickled
    ginger, well drained
2 bowls warm cooked rice

Note: If you can't find mitsuba (also known as Japanese parsley and other names), try substituting mizuna greens, Italian parsley, chervil or celery leaves.

1 Remove the meat from the chicken wings and shred roughly. Chop up the mitsuba or other greens into 1¼ in (3 cm) pieces. Finely shred the pickled ginger.

2 Put the rice, chicken and mitsuba in a large bowl and mix well. Serve in individual rice bowls.

Because the chicken wings are cooked thoroughly, the meat just falls off the bones. Remove the cartilage as well as the bones, to make this easy to eat.

Simmered Beef and Tofu

This classic simmered dish has a salty-sweet flavor like sukiyaki. It's great with plain rice or as a snack while drinking. If you want it to be even more flavorful, let it cool down before eating.

Prevent the beef from getting too tough by adding it later. Take care not to overcook the tofu, or the texture will become rough and unpleasant.

Serves 2

1 block firm tofu, about 8 oz (250 g)
4 thin green onions (scallions)
5 oz (125 g) thinly sliced beef

For the simmering liquid
⅔ cup (160 ml) kombu dashi stock
2½ tablespoons dark soy sauce
2 tablespoons raw sugar
1½ tablespoons sake

1. Cut the tofu into 8 pieces. Slice the green onions into 3 in (8 cm) diagonal pieces.

2. Put all the simmering liquid ingredients in a pan and bring to a boil over medium heat. Add the tofu and simmer for about 4 minutes. Add the beef and simmer for a further 3 minutes. Add the green onions at the end, and simmer briefly.

Shabu Shabu Salad

During the hot summer months, I often get a craving for this cold version of shabu shabu, a dish where thin pork slices are cooked briefly in hot water and eaten with a sauce. This cooking method ensures the pork is tender.

To ensure tender pork, cook quickly in hot but not boiling water. Take it out while it's still a bit pink—it will continue cooking with residual heat.

Serves 2

6 very thin pork slices, about 7 oz (200 g)
1 medium tomato, for garnish
Handful mizuna greens, or other greens, for garnish

For the sesame sauce
1 tablespoon tahini, or sesame paste
2 teaspoons dark soy sauce
1 tablespoon rice vinegar
Pinch of raw sugar

1. Bring a pan of water to a boil, then turn off the heat. Separate the pork slices and put one slice in the hot water at a time and spread them out. Move each slice around in the water with a fork; when the pork turns a pale pink but not quite grey, take it out, place in a colander or sieve lined with a paper towel and leave to cool. (If you want the pork to be really chilled, refrigerate it for a while.)

2. Make a crisscross shallow cut into the flat end of the tomato, dunk it into boiling water and peel off the skin. Cut the tomato into 8 wedges. Cut the greens into 2 in (5 cm) long pieces.

3. Put the sesame sauce ingredients in a bowl and mix well.

4. Arrange the pork, tomatoes and mizuna greens on plates and spoon over the sesame sauce.

Japanese-style Beef Steak

Steak is a treat for special occasions. I'm sure there are plenty of people who would like to learn how to cook a piece of expensive beef properly. In this recipe I'll share with you my secret for cooking steak so that it's not over- or under-done.

Note: Yuzu kosho is a condiment made with ground green chili peppers, yuzu juice and zest. It is spicy, slightly sour and refreshing. It's sold in jars and is available at Japanese grocery stores or online.

Serves 2

2 beef steaks
Salt and pepper
Olive oil
Green beans, strings removed, trimmed
3 king oyster mushrooms, sliced in half
Salt and pepper, to taste
Yuzu kosho (see Note), to taste

If cooking rare or medium rare steaks, bring meat that has been refrigerated to room temperature before cooking. Cover the steaks while they come to room temperature to prevent them from drying out.

Give the steaks a mouthwatering brown surface by pan-frying them over high heat. A cast-iron frying pan is perfect for browning the meat evenly. When you put the steaks in the pan, don't move them around for while. The steaks are done if they bounce back slightly when pressed with a finger.

Once fried, wrap the two steaks in a piece of foil for 3 to 4 minutes so they continue to cook with residual heat. The steak in the photo is about ½ in (about 1.5 cm) thick. If your steaks are thicker than that, leave them wrapped for 5 to 8 minutes.

1 Leave the steaks out for 2 to 3 hours until the meat no longer feels cold to the touch. Season with salt and pepper on both sides just before cooking.

2 Heat a frying pan (preferably a cast-iron one) over high heat, spread around some olive oil, and add the seasoned steaks. Turn the heat to medium-high and fry until the meat has changed color about one fifth of the way up the sides. Turn the steaks and fry on the other side. If your steaks are very thick, quickly sear the sides too.

3 Take the steaks out of the pan and wrap in aluminum foil. Rest for 3 to 4 minutes.

4 Heat more olive oil in the same frying pan. Put in the green beans and king oyster mushrooms and stir-fry. Season with salt and pepper. Remove from the pan, cut the green beans in half and cut the king oyster mushrooms into bite-size pieces; arrange both on two serving plates. Slice the steaks into slices and arrange on the plates. Serve a little yuzu kosho on the side.

VARIATION

Sauté the onion slowly to bring out its sweetness, until it's a light golden brown as shown in the photo.

White Wine and Onion Sauce

Bring out the flavors of steak with a rich, sweet sauce.

Serves 2

2 teaspoons
  unsalted butter
½ onion, finely
  chopped
½ tablespoon
  olive oil
2 beef steaks
2 tablespoons
  white wine
Salt and pepper
Chopped parsley

1 Heat the butter in a frying pan, add the onion and sauté over medium-low heat until slightly browned. Take the onion and butter out of the pan.

2 Add the olive oil to the same frying pan. Fry the steaks, following Steps 1 and 2 of the recipe above.

3 Discard any remaining fat in the pan. Put in the wine and stir over medium heat while scraping the pan with a spatula. Put the onion back in and sauté until golden brown. Season with salt and pepper.

4 Put the steaks on serving plates, and spoon the onion sauce over them. Sprinkle with chopped parsley and serve.

Simmered Yellowtail and Daikon

This classic wintertime dish is known as *buri daikon*. The daikon radish, which soaks up the umami of the fish, is particularly tasty. If you can get your hands on yellowtail bones, throw them into the simmering pot too for even more flavor. Use swordfish if you can't find yellowtail.

ust like mackerel or other oily fish,
ellowtail has a pretty strong fishy odor.
Pouring boiling water over will eliminate
he fishiness. Don't skip this important
tep. See page 17 (Mackerel in Miso
auce) for more detailed instructions.

aikon radish isn't bitter, so you can
microwave it instead of parboiling. Put the slices
n a microwave-safe plate, cover with cling film
nd microwave at 600W for about 5 minutes.

Serves 2

2 pieces fresh yellowtail,
 or swordfish, each about
 6–8 oz (150–250 g)
Salt, for sprinkling
1¼ lb (600 g) daikon radish,
 peeled
1 piece ginger root, peeled
 and thinly sliced

For the simmering liquid
2 tablespoons soy sauce
½ cup (125 ml) sake
1½ tablespoons mirin
1 tablespoon sugar
1¼ cups (300 ml) water

Garnishes
Finely shredded ginger

1 Cut each piece of fish in half, and sprinkle salt on both sides. Leave to rest for 10 minutes. Put the fish pieces on a shallow sieve or in a colander and pour boiling water over them until the surface is white. Briefly put the fish in a bowl of cold water, then drain and pat dry with paper towels.

2 Slice the daikon radish into ¾ in (2 cm) thick slices, then cut each slice into quarters. Put into a pan with cold water to cover, bring to a boil and boil for about 8 minutes, then drain into a colander.

3 Put the daikon radish, sliced ginger and all the simmering liquid ingredients in a pan. Cover with a small lid that sits right on top of the ingredients in a pan, or a piece of kitchen parchment paper with several holes poked into it. Bring to a boil over medium heat, and add the fish. Cover again, and simmer over low heat for about 15 minutes. Serve with a little shredded ginger.

VARIATION

Yellowtail with Miso Butter Sauce

The sweet, thick sauce goes surprisingly well with the yellowtail.

Serves 2

2 pieces fresh yellowtail,
 or swordfish, each about
 6–8 oz (150–250 g)
Salt, for sprinkling
1¼ lb (600 g) daikon
 radish, peeled
1 piece ginger root, peeled
 and thinly sliced

For the simmering liquid
½ cup (125 ml) sake
1¼ cups (300 ml) water
3 tablespoons white miso
 paste
1½ tablespoons unsalted
 butter
1 teaspoon cornstarch
1 teaspoon water

Garnishes
Grated yuzu or
 lemon zest
 (optional)

1 Follow Steps 1 and 2 of the recipe for Simmered Yellowtail and Daikon Radish (above).

2 Put the daikon radish, sliced ginger and the sake and water from the simmering liquid ingredients into a pan over medium heat. When it comes to a boil, add the fish. Lower the heat to medium-low, and simmer for about 10 minutes.

3 Add the miso and butter, and simmer for another 5 minutes.

4 Mix the cornstarch and 1 teaspoon of water together. Turn off the heat under the pan, swirl in the cornstarch-and-water mixture and stir quickly. Turn the heat back on to low, and simmer until the sauce is thickened. Turn off the heat. Serve topped with grated yuzu or lemon zest.

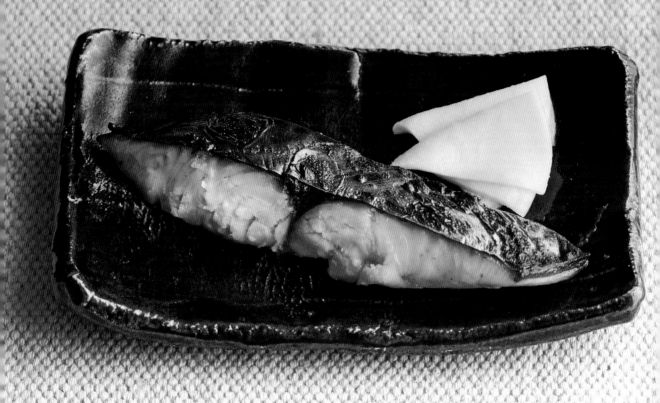

Miso-marinated Mackerel

Marinate the fish in advance, cook it and you have your main dish! This marinating method also works well with salmon, cod, chicken and pork. Mild white miso goes well with mackerel, but you can change the miso type depending on what you are marinating.

The longer the fish is marinated, the deeper the flavor will be. You can also freeze the fish, wrapped in the marinade, for up to 3 weeks.

Serves 2

2 pieces Spanish mackerel,
  or 2 salmon fillets
A little salt
Pickles or greens, for garnish

For the miso marinade
⅓ cup (100 g) white miso
2 teaspoons sake
2 teaspoons mirin

1. Salt both sides of the fish pieces, and rest for about 20 minutes. Wipe off any moisture that comes out of the fish with paper towels.

2. Put the miso marinade ingredients in a bowl, and mix well to combine.

3. Spread the marinade on a sheet of cling film. Put the fish pieces on top of the marinade and spread the top sides of the fish with more marinade. Wrap the fish tightly so it is completely enveloped in the marinade. Refrigerate at least overnight, or for up to 3 days.

4. Unwrap the fish and wipe off the marinade. Rinse it quickly under running water and pat dry with paper towels. Cook on a heated grill (use a fish grill if you have one), or bake in a 400°F (200°C) oven until lightly browned. Here I've served with pickled turnip (available at Japanese groceries), but you can use a few sprigs of watercress, parsley or baby greens instead.

Crunchy Shrimp Fritters

Flavorful shrimp paste is sandwiched between crunchy slices of lotus root. The shrimp filling is subtly flavored with ginger juice and shiso leaves.

Serves 2

oz (100 g) fresh shrimp, peeled and cleaned
little ginger juice (grate some ginger and
  squeeze out the juice)
green shiso leaves or basil leaves
alt, to taste

Section of fresh lotus root,
  about 2 in (5 cm) long
Cornstarch, for dusting
Oil, for deep-frying
1 lime

1 Chop up the shrimp roughly, then go over it again with a knife to chop it into a paste. Put the shrimp paste in a bowl with the ginger juice, finely chopped green shiso or basil leaves and salt, and mix well.

2 Wash and peel the lotus root section, then slice it into 8 rounds, each about ¼ in (6 mm) thick. Dust the slices thoroughly on both sides with cornstarch. Spread one quarter of the shrimp paste onto a slice of lotus root, and top with another slice to make a sandwich. Dust the surface of the shrimp paste between the slices with cornstarch too.

3 Put some oil in a pan or deep frying pan, and heat to 340°F (170°C). Put in the lotus root–shrimp sandwiches and deep-fry until crispy and light brown, turning once. Cut each slice in half and serve with half a lime.

Steamed Sea Bream

Fish steamed with kombu seaweed has a lighter flavor than simmered fish. The key is to steam the fish fast over high heat. The fish will turn out tender, juicy and flavorful.

Serves 2

2 pieces sea bream, or similar white fish
Salt, for sprinkling
Handful shimeji mushrooms, or other flavorful
   mushrooms of your choice
4 in (10 cm) square piece dried kombu seaweed
2 tablespoons sake
Yuzu or lime zest, shredded, for garnish
Ponzu sauce, to taste

Note: If you don't have a steamer, use a steamer basket that fits inside a regular pan, or a bamboo steamer from an Asian kitchen-supply store. Or try this: Find an ovenproof plate just a bit smaller than one of your pans. Put 3–4 crumpled up balls of aluminum foil in the pan. Put in water so that it comes to about halfway up the balls. Put the fish and mushrooms on the plate, and place inside the pan on top of the balls. Put a lid on the pan and bring the water to a boil. Open the lid halfway, and continue steaming until the fish and mushrooms are done, about 7 minutes.

1. Sprinkle both sides of the fish with salt, and rest for 15 minutes. Wipe off any moisture that comes out of the fish with paper towel. Make several shallow cuts into the skin side of the fish.

2. Cut the tough stem ends off the shimeji mushrooms. Line a heatproof dish with the kombu seaweed, and place the fish and mushrooms on top. Sprinkle with the sake.

3. Bring a food steamer or steaming machine (see Note) to full heat so that the steam is rising briskly. Put the dish with the fish and mushrooms in the steamer, and steam over high heat for 6 to 7 minutes. Transfer to serving plates and top with some finely shredded yuzu zest. Sprinkle on ponzu sauce before eating.

Sardines in Plum Sauce

Tart pickled plums go well with sardines.

Serves 2

6 fresh sardines
2 umeboshi pickled plums
1 piece ginger, thinly sliced

For the simmering liquid
2½ tablespoons dark soy sauce
⅔ cup (160 ml) sake
2½ tablespoons mirin
⅔ cup (160 ml) water

1 Scrape the scales off the sardines with the tip of a knife, and cut off the heads and tails. Open up the belly side and remove the intestines. Rinse under running water and pat dry. (See page 56 for detailed instructions.)

2 Put all the simmering liquid ingredients in a pan over medium heat and bring to a boil. Add the umeboshi pickled plums and ginger. Put the sardines into the pan in a single layer, and cover with a small lid that fits right on top of the fish, or a piece of kitchen parchment paper with a few holes poked in it. Simmer over medium-low heat.

3 When the liquid in the pan has reduced by half, take the lid off and continue simmering while swirling the pan to coat the fish with the sauce. When there is just a little liquid left in the pan and the sardines are shiny, turn the heat off. Transfer the sardines and the remaining liquid to a serving plate.

Braised Flounder

If you can't find flounder, use a similar flat fish. The key is to use lots of sake in the simmering liquid.

Serves 2

2 pieces flounder or similar flat fish, such as halibut, plaice or sole

For the simmering liquid
3 tablespoons dark soy sauce
¾ cup (185 ml) sake
3 tablespoons mirin
1 tablespoon raw sugar
Mint leaves, or kinome (sansho pepper leaves), for garnish

1 Scrape the scales off the fish with the tip of a knife. Make several shallow cuts into the skin side.

2 Place the fish in a colander, and pour boiling water over it to "frost" it (turn the surface white).

3 Put the simmering liquid ingredients in a pan over medium heat. When the liquid comes to a boil, add the fish, skin side up, and cover with a small lid that fits right on top of the fish, or with a piece of kitchen parchment paper with a few holes poked in it. Cook over medium-high heat for about 10 minutes.

4 Take off the lid, and continue cooking while swirling the pan to coat the fish with the sauce. When there is very little liquid left in the pan, turn off the heat. Serve garnished with mint leaves or kinome.

Sweet and Sour Mackerel

The traditional sweet-sour sauce used to make this dish is called *nanban-su* (vinegar from southern lands). Fish cooked this way is so good that you can't stop eating it! I've added dashi stock to this recipe too, for an even deeper flavor.

If you fry small fish like this at high temperature until lightly browned and crispy, you can eat the whole fish, including the heads, tails and bones. This extended frying process also gives the fish a lovely nutty flavor.

As soon as you drain the oil from the fish, put them directly into the shallow tray with the nanban vinegar sauce. If you let the fish get cold before putting them in, they won't soak up the flavors well. Cover the fish with the onion slices to help the flavors penetrate.

Serves 2

½ medium onion
12 small horse mackerel or baby sardines, 8 oz (250 g) total
Flour, for dusting
Oil, for deep-frying

For the sauce
1¼ cups (300 ml) dashi stock (see pages 6–7)
2½ tablespoons light soy sauce
2 tablespoons mirin
3 tablespoons rice vinegar
1½ tablespoons sugar
¼–½ red chili pepper, deseeded and sliced

1 Slice the onion thinly. Combine all the sauce ingredients in a bowl, and mix until the sugar is dissolved. Transfer the sauce to a shallow tray, and add the onion.

2 Open up the Spanish mackerel from the belly side and remove the intestines (see page 56). Rinse under running water and pat dry. Dust lightly with flour.

3 Put some oil in a pan or deep frying pan and heat to 355°F (180°C). Add the floured fish and fry, turning occasionally, until crispy on the surface. Take out and drain off the oil.

4 Put the hot just-fried fish in the sauce. Leave to marinate for 30 minutes before serving, turning once during that time.

VARIATION

Mackerel with Peppers

This variation on Sweet and Sour Mackerel uses colorful red and yellow bell peppers.

Serves 2

⅓ each red and yellow bell peppers, deseeded
¼ celery stalk
12 small horse mackerel or baby sardines, 8 oz (250 g) total
Flour
Oil, for deep-frying

For the sauce
1 teaspoon light soy sauce
1 tablespoon lemon juice
3 tablespoons white wine vinegar
2 teaspoons honey
½ teaspoon salt
3 tablespoons olive oil

1 Slice the bell peppers thinly. Blanch in hot water (see page 28 for how to blanch), and drain. Remove the tough outer fibers of the celery and shred lengthwise. Combine all the sauce ingredients in a bowl and mix. Transfer to a shallow tray, and add the bell pepper and celery.

2 Follow Steps 2 to 4 of the Sweet and Sour Mackerel recipe above.

Mixed Tempura Fritters

You'll be surprised at how easy it can be to cook tempura. All you need to do is pay attention to a few small points. The more you make this dish, the easier it gets, and you can enjoy cooking seasonal ingredients tempura-style all year round!

Make several small, deep diagonal cuts into the belly side of each shrimp to sever the sinew and straighten out the shrimp. It should now hang down straight when you hold it by the tail.

Mix the batter briefly once you have lifted in the flour. It's fine if a few floury lumps remain. If you overmix the batter, it won't be crispy when fried. Another key is to chill the batter ingredients and the bowl beforehand.

Serves 2 or 4

8 large fresh shrimp
1½ in piece Asian or
    regular sweet potato
    (see Note)
12 green beans
½ medium onion
Flour, for dusting
Oil, for deep-frying

For the fritter batter
1 egg yolk
¾ cup (185 ml) cold water
1 cup (120 g) flour

For the dipping sauce
¾ cup (185 ml) dashi
    stock (see pages 6–7)
2½ tablespoons soy
    sauce
2½ tablespoons mirin
Grated daikon radish
Grated ginger

Note: Asian sweet potatoes have purple skin and pale creamy flesh, and are sweeter and less watery than the orange type of sweet potato. I recommend the Asian type if you can find them, but either type works fine.

1. Refrigerate the tempura batter ingredients and all the items to be coated in the batter until just before you use them.

2. Shell the shrimp, leaving the tail on. Remove the intestines (see page 56). Make a cut into the end of each shrimp tail, and scrape a knife tip towards the end to push out the water in the tail. Rinse the shrimp in lightly salted cold water, and pat dry. Make 3 to 4 small deep cuts in the belly side of each shrimp, hold them at the back side, and straighten them out.

3. Slice the sweet potato into 4 rounds, leaving the skin on. Remove the strings from the green beans. Slice the onion thinly against the grain, about ¼ in (6 mm) thick. Skewer the onion slices with wooden toothpicks to prevent the rings from separating.

4. Make the fritter batter. Put the egg yolk and cold water in a chilled bowl and mix together. Sift in the flour and mix roughly.

5. Dust the ingredients to be fried lightly with flour, using a brush. This will ensure that the batter doesn't come off them while frying.

6. Put some oil in a pan or deep frying pan, and heat to 340°F (170°C). Dip the flour-dusted ingredients in the batter, and fry, a couple of pieces at a time, turning each piece once or twice, until crispy. Drain off the oil.

7. Put all the dipping sauce ingredients in a pan and bring to a boil. Arrange the tempura on plates and serve with the dipping sauce in a bowl on the side. Grated daikon radish and grated ginger can be served to mix into the dipping sauce.

VARIATION

Slide each fritter into the hot oil slowly, at the side of the pan, using a ladle. If it looks as if it will fall apart, hold it for a few seconds until it firms.

Scallop Fritters

Lotus root adds an amazingly crunchy texture!

Makes 8 Fritters

4–5 large fresh scallops
Small bunch parsley, or mitsuba
1 lotus root, about 4 oz (100 g),
    peeled
Flour, for dusting

Oil, for frying
Salt, to serve

For the fritter batter
As above

1. Cut the scallops into ½ in (1 cm) dice. Slice the parsley into 1¼ in (3 cm) pieces. Cut the lotus root into ¼ in (6 mm) thick slices, then cut each slice into small wedges.

2. Make the fritter batter, following the instructions in Step 4 of the recipe above.

3. Put the scallops, parsley and lotus root in a bowl, and dust lightly with flour.

4. Make ready a separate small bowl, and put in ⅛ of the batter. Add ⅛ of the mixture from Step 3 into the batter and mix. (When you tilt the bowl a small amount of batter should remain at the bottom.)

5. Put some oil in a pan or deep frying pan, and heat to 340°F (170°C). Scoop up the contents of the small bowl with a spoon or small ladle, and slide into the oil along the side of the pan. When the fritter has firmed up, turn it over, and fry until crispy. Repeat steps 4 and 5 for the rest of the batter and ingredients. Serve on a plate with salt on the side.

How to Prepare Seafood

Clams

Put the clams in a shallow bowl, and add enough salt water (1 tablespoon of salt per 2 cups water) to cover. Put on a lid and leave to soak for 2–3 hours. Rinse with plain water before using.

Shrimp

Shell the shrimp and make a shallow cut into the back side to remove the veins (photo a). If you don't want to make a cut in the shrimp, make a hole in the back with a bamboo skewer and pull the veins out (photo b).

Squid

1. Hold the squid around its eyes, and pull the innards out of the body.

2. Pull out the plastic-like quill from the body.

3. To prepare the legs, make a cut under the eyes. Remove the hard beak in the middle of the legs. Discard the eye and innards.

4. To prepare the body, insert your fingers between the body and the side fins and pull to separate them. Discard the fins.

Sardines

1. Scrape off the scales with the tip of a knife. Cut off the head.

2. Cut into the belly side, and remove the intestines. Rinse the fish and pat dry.

3. Insert your thumbs along the spine and open up the fish to the tail.

4. Remove the spine, starting from the head end.

5. Shave off the hard spiny part near the tail with a knife.

Mackerel

1. Use the tip of a knife to scrape off the scales. Shave off the hard spiny part near the tail.

2. Cut off the head.

3. Cut open the belly, and remove the intestines. Rinse the fish and pat dry.

4. Cut into the back side, and run your knife parallel to the cutting board along the spine, from the head end to the tail.

5. Cut into the tail end towards the back. Feel the knife hitting the spine, and move your knife slowly towards the head while opening up the fish.

6. Insert the knife tip between the spine and the body, and cut off that half of the fish. You now have one fillet.

7. Repeat on the other side to remove the other fillet.

8. Cut off the bones on the belly side.

9. Pull out any small bones, using tweezers.

10. Finished. You will have two boned fillets, plus the spine part.

CHAPTER 3
Everyday Side Dishes

These side dishes are great supporting players that are indispensable to everyday meals. They are mainly vegetable based, and also include eggs and tofu. I have included dishes that can be made in advance and stocked in the refrigerator, and items that work well in bento lunch boxes too.

Daikon Radish with Chicken-Miso Sauce

Cut the daikon radish into thick, hearty slices to enjoy the texture. If you overcook kombu seaweed the flavor is ruined, so take it out as soon as the water comes to a boil.

Serves 2 as a side dish

1 piece dried kombu seaweed, 4 x 2 in (10 x 5 cm)
2 cups (500 ml) water
2 slices daikon radish, 2 in (5 cm) thick
3 tablespoons sake
1 tablespoon mirin
2 blanched snow peas, for garnish

For the sauce
2 tablespoons ground chicken
1 tablespoon sake
3 tablespoons miso
1 tablespoon sugar
1 tablespoon mirin
1 teaspoon ginger juice (grate ginger and squeeze out the juice)

The hot daikon radish is packed with the umami of the dashi stock.

1. Put the kombu seaweed and 2 cups of water in a pan, and leave to soak for at least 2 hours.

2. Peel the daikon radish thickly, and shave the sharp corners off the cut sides. Make a crisscross cut into the center of one cut side of each piece.

3. Put the daikon radish pieces in the pan, and bring to a boil over medium heat. Take out the kombu seaweed once the pan comes to a boil and add the sake and mirin. Turn the heat to low and simmer the daikon radish until a bamboo skewer goes through the middle of a piece easily.

4. Make the sauce. Put the ground chicken and sake in a pan over medium heat, and cook while stirring until there is almost no moisture left in the pan. Add the miso, sugar and mirin and mix until smooth with a wooden spatula. When the sauce is shiny, add the ginger juice and mix.

5. Put each daikon piece on a plate. Top with the sauce and garnish with snow peas cut in half diagonally.

Stir-fried Spicy Root Vegetables

These vegetable matchsticks are so crunchy!

Serves 2 to 3 as a side dish

1 burdock root (optional)
½ carrot (or 1 large carrot if not using burdock)
2 teaspoons dark sesame oil
½ red chili pepper, sliced into thin rounds
1 tablespoon soy sauce
1 tablespoon sake
1 tablespoon mirin
2 teaspoons raw sugar
2 teaspoons roasted white sesame seeds

1. Lightly scrub the skin off the burdock root, if using, with a stiff vegetable brush or a wad of crumpled up aluminum foil, and rinse. Cut into 2½ in (6 cm) long matchsticks, place in a bowl of cold water, soak for 5 minutes and drain. Cut the carrot in the same way.

2. Heat the sesame oil in a frying pan and add the burdock, carrot and red chili pepper. Stir-fry over medium heat.

3. When the vegetables are slightly wilted, add the soy sauce, sake, mirin and sugar and continue stir-frying until there is no moisture left in the pan. Turn the heat off and add the sesame seeds. Mix briefly and transfer to a serving bowl.

Eggplant with Miso Sauce

This sweet and salty miso topping is called *dengaku* sauce in Japan, and is great with vegetables or tofu.

Serves 2 as a side dish

2 small Asian eggplants, or ½ large eggplant
2 tablespoons vegetable oil
Roasted white sesame seeds

For the miso sauce
2 tablespoons red miso paste
1 tablespoon sake
2 teaspoons mirin
3 tablespoons raw sugar

1. Put the sauce ingredients in a pan over low heat. Cook while mixing constantly for about 3 minutes, until the sauce has thickened.

2. Cut the eggplants into 1¼ in (3 cm) thick slices. Soak briefly in cold water and drain; pat dry. Put the eggplant slices in a bowl, add the vegetable oil and toss to coat.

3. Heat a frying pan, put in the eggplant slices and fry on both sides over medium heat. When both sides are browned, cover the pan with a lid, turn the heat down to low and steam-fry for 2 to 3 minutes.

4. Arrange the eggplant slices on a plate, spoon on the miso sauce and sprinkle with sesame seeds.

Tofu with Greens

This dish uses komatsuna greens, but you can use any greens you like.

Serves 2 to 3 as a side dish

1 piece thin-fried tofu (aburaage)
1 bunch komatsuna, or spinach
¾ cup (185 ml) dashi stock (see pages 6–7)
2 teaspoons light soy sauce
1½ tablespoons mirin

1. Put the aburaage in a colander and pour boiling water over it to remove the oil on the surface. Drain well. Cut in half lengthwise, then into ½ in (1 cm) wide strips. Trim the roots from the greens and cut into 1½ in (4 cm) lengths.

2. Put the dashi, light soy sauce and mirin in a pan over medium heat. When the pan comes to a boil, add the stem parts of the greens and the aburaage. Simmer for 2 to 3 minutes. When the stems have wilted, add the leaf parts and simmer briefly.

Simmered Tofu

Use a generous amount of simmering liquid for a moist finish.

Serves 2 to 4 as a side dish

2 dried shiitake mushrooms
A few strips konnyaku (optional), about 2 oz (50 g)
2 pieces thin-fried tofu (aburaage)
½ carrot
1 tablespoon dark sesame oil
7 oz (200 g) fresh okara soy pulp, or firm tofu blended in a food processor to a creamy consistency
2 cups (500 ml) dashi stock (see pages 6–7)
2 tablespoons light soy sauce
2 tablespoons sake
4 teaspoons sugar

1. Soak the shiitake in hot water for about 20 minutes until softened. Cut off and discard the stems and slice the caps thinly. If using konnyaku, slice into thin strips, pour boiling water over the strips and drain. Pour boiling water over the aburaage, drain and cut into thin strips. Slice the carrot into matchsticks.

2. Heat the sesame oil in a pan. Add all the ingredients from Step 1 and stir-fry over medium heat. When the carrots and mushrooms have wilted, add the okara soy pulp and mix briefly.

3. Add the dashi, light soy sauce, sake and sugar to the pan. Simmer over low heat, stirring occasionally, until almost no moisture is left in the pan.

pinach in Dashi

njoy the delicious flavors of spinach
nd dashi stock.

Tofu Side Salad

This simple and tasty tofu side dish is a
Japanese classic.

Serves 2 to 3 as a side dish

4 cup (185 ml) dashi stock (see pages 6–7)
tablespoon light soy sauce
tablespoon mirin
bunch spinach, about 7 oz (200 g)
inch of salt
bowl of ice water
onito flakes, for garnish (optional)

1. Make the sauce by combining the dashi, light soy sauce and mirin in a pan. Bring to a boil over medium heat, transfer to another container and leave to cool.

2. Wash the spinach in a bowl filled with water. Bring a generous amount of water to a boil in a pan, and add a pinch of salt. Holding the whole bunch of spinach, put in the root and stem part only into the boiling water and hold for 20 seconds. Put the whole bunch of spinach into the water and boil for another minute. Drain, put the spinach into a bowl of ice water, then drain again and squeeze out the excess water well.

3. Put the sauce from Step 1 into a shallow tray, put in the cooked spinach, and refrigerate for an hour.

4. Take the spinach out and squeeze lightly. Cut into 2 in (5 cm) pieces. Arrange in serving bowls and spoon on a little sauce. Top with a few bonito flakes.

Serves 2 as a side dish

1 block firm tofu, about 7 oz (200 g)
2 tablespoons tahini, or sesame paste
2 tablespoons dashi stock (see pages 6–7)
2 teaspoons light soy sauce
2 teaspoons sugar
1 piece konnyaku (optional), about 3 oz (75 g)
¼ carrot
Large handful of spinach
½ cup (125 ml) dashi stock
2 teaspoons light soy sauce
1 teaspoon mirin

1. Drain the tofu, following the instructions on page 80. Put the tofu in a large mortar or grinding bowl, and grind with a pestle until smooth. Add the tahini, the 2 tablespoons of dashi, 2 teaspoons of light soy sauce and sugar, and continue grinding and mixing.

2. Cut the konnyaku, if using, into small strips, boil briefly and drain. Cut the carrot into matchsticks. Briefly boil the spinach in salted water, drain, cool in ice water, drain again and squeeze out firmly. Cut into 1¼ in (3 cm) pieces.

3. Put the ½ cup dashi, 2 teaspoons light soy sauce, and 1 teaspoon mirin in a pan and bring to a boil over medium heat. Add the carrot and konnyaku and simmer for 2 to 3 minutes. When the carrot is tender, add the spinach and simmer briefly.

4. Drain the ingredients from Step 3, and mix them with the tofu mixture from Step 1.

Deep-fried Tofu Dumplings with Shrimp

Freshly fried, these tofu dumplings are a great snack with drinks.

So that the dumplings don't break while frying, press firmly when forming into balls to eliminate air pockets.

Makes 10 dumplings

Block of firm tofu, about 10 oz (300 g)
4 oz (100 g) fresh shrimp, peeled
10 dried wood ear mushrooms
1 small edible lily bulb (optional)
20 fresh or canned gingko nuts
½ beaten egg
Salt, to taste
1 oz (30 g) nagaimo yam (or regular potato), grated
Oil, for deep-frying
Grated ginger, to serve
Soy sauce, to serve

Note: Find edible lily bulbs (*yurine* in Japanese) and nagaimo yam at Asian grocery stores. Fresh gingko nuts may be available in season at Asian grocery stores, or you can gather them under gingko trees. Also find canned ready-cooked gingko nuts at Japanese grocery stores.

1. Drain the tofu, following the instructions on page 80.

2. Devein the shrimp if they are not yet cleaned (see page 56), and chop up roughly. Soak the wood ear mushrooms for 15–30 minutes until soft, remove any tough parts and shred. Separate the lily bulb sections, if using, and cut into bite-size pieces. If using fresh gingko nuts, dry-roast them in a frying pan until the shells split, then peel.

3. Put the tofu in a mortar or grinding bowl, and grind with a pestle until smooth. Add the beaten egg and salt and continue mixing and grinding. When everything is well combined, add the ingredients from Step 2 and the nagaimo yam or potato, and mix. Divide the mixture into 10 portions and form each portion into balls.

4. Put some oil in a pan or deep frying pan, and heat to 340°F (170°C). Put in the balls a few at a time and deep-fry until a light golden brown. Take out and drain off the oil. Serve with grated ginger and soy sauce on the side.

Simmered Squash

This has a delicious, slightly sweet taste.

1½ cups (300 g) cubed butternut
  or kabocha squash, seeds and
  pith removed
2 cups (500 ml) water
1 piece dried kombu seaweed,
  4 x 2 in (10 x 5 cm)
2 tablespoons mirin
2 tablespoons light soy sauce

1. If using butternut squash, peel. If using kabocha, peel the skin randomly in some places.

2. Put the squash in a single layer in a pan. Add the 2 cups water and kombu seaweed to the pan and turn the heat to medium. When the water comes to a boil, remove the kombu, and cover the pan with a small lid that fits right on top of the squash, or a piece of kitchen parchment paper with a few holes poked in it. Simmer over low heat for about 10 minutes.

3. When a bamboo skewer goes easily through a piece of squash, add the mirin and simmer for an additional 3 minutes. Add the soy sauce and simmer for another 3 minutes. Turn off the heat and leave as-is until cool, so that the squash absorbs all the flavors.

Taro Root in Soy Sauce

The dense, sticky texture of this dish is deeply satisfying.

20 Japanese taro roots (satoimo), or
  8 oz (250 g) regular taro root
1¾ cups (425 ml) dashi stock (see pages 6–7)
3 tablespoons mirin
2½ tablespoons soy sauce

1. Peel the taro roots, and rinse quickly in water. If using regular taro root, cut into bite-size pieces.

2. Put the dashi and taro roots in a pan over medium heat. Bring to a boil and add the mirin. Cover with a small lid that fits right on top of the taro roots, or a piece of kitchen parchment paper with a few holes poked in it. Simmer over medium-low heat for about 15 minutes.

3. When a bamboo skewer goes easily through a taro root, add the soy sauce and simmer over low heat until there is almost no moisture left in the pan.

Octopus and Cucumber in Vinegar Sauce

This mildly sour sauce is made using sugar and dashi.

Daikon and Carrot Salad

Dried fruit adds sweetness to this slightly sour vegetable dish.

Serves 2 as a side dish

1 Japanese cucumber, or ½ English
  cucumber
¼ teaspoon salt
2 oz (60 g) boiled octopus (available at
  Japanese markets)
½ cup (125 ml) dashi stock
⅔ cup (160 ml) rice vinegar
1 tablespoon light soy sauce
½ tablespoon raw sugar
Small piece ginger, peeled and shredded

1. Slice the cucumber thinly. Sprinkle with the salt and rub it in with your hands. Leave for 5 minutes, and squeeze out tightly to eliminate excess moisture.

2. Cut the octopus into bite-size pieces.

3. Put the dashi, vinegar, light soy sauce and sugar in a bowl and mix. Just before serving, add the ginger to the bowl, then the cucumber and octopus. Mix and serve.

Serves 2 to 3 as a side dish

⅓ cup (80 ml) rice vinegar
3 tablespoons sugar
½ teaspoon salt
Piece daikon radish, about 4 oz (100 g), peeled
Small piece of carrot
Pinch of salt
1 dried persimmon, or other dried fruit
A little shredded yuzu or lemon zest (optional)

1. Put the vinegar, sugar and ½ teaspoon salt in a par over medium heat. Stir until the sugar has dissolve and turn off the heat. Leave to cool.

2. Finely shred the daikon and the carrot. Put them into a bowl with the pinch of salt and rub the salt in. Leave for 5 minutes, then squeeze tightly to remove excess moisture.

3. Cut the dried fruit into thin strips.

4. Combine the vegetables and dried fruit in a bowl. Add the vinegar sauce from Step 1 and mix well. Add a little shredded yuzu or lemon zest if you like mix quickly and serve.

Pan-fried Mushrooms

I use shiitake, shimeji and maitake
mushrooms but use any type you like.

Green Beans with Sesame Sauce

Use freshly roasted sesame seeds for
maximum fragrance and flavor.

Serves 2 as a side dish

cup (160 ml) dashi stock (see pages 6–7)
teaspoons mirin
teaspoons light soy sauce
iece daikon radish, about 4 oz (100 g), peeled
fresh shiitake mushrooms*
andful shimeji mushrooms, about 2 oz (50 g)*
iece maitake mushroom, about 2 oz (50 g)*
(*substitute with mushrooms of your choice)
il, for frying

1. Combine the dashi, mirin and light soy sauce in a pan.
   Bring to a boil over medium heat. Transfer to a bowl
   and leave to cool.

2. Grate the daikon radish and drain off any excess
   moisture. Add to the sauce made in Step 1.

3. Remove and discard the stems from the shiitake, if
   using, and slice the caps thinly. Cut the stem ends off
   the shimeji mushrooms, if using, and break apart into
   small clumps. Break the maitake mushroom, if using,
   into easy-to-eat pieces.

4. Heat a little oil in a frying pan, add the mushrooms and
   fry while turning occasionally until browned. Add the
   bowl of sauce from Step 2, and mix.

Serves 2 as a side dish

4 oz (100 g) green beans
3 tablespoons white sesame seeds
A little dashi stock (see pages 6–7)
2 teaspoons mirin
1 teaspoon soy sauce
1 tablespoon sugar

1. Remove the strings from the green beans and boil
   them for 2 to 3 minutes in lightly salted water (so
   they are still al dente). Drain, refresh in cold water,
   and drain again. Cut each green bean into 3 pieces.

2. Toast the sesame seeds in a dry frying pan, and grind
   them in a mortar or grinding bowl using a pestle.

3. Add the dashi, mirin, soy sauce and sugar to the
   ground sesame seeds and mix. Add the green beans
   and mix well.

Steamed Savory Custard

Called *chawan mushi* in Japanese, this can take the place of soup in a meal.

steam over high heat until the surface is firm, then turn the heat to low and cook slowly. This is the key to a smooth custard.

Serves 2

⅓ boneless chicken thigh, about 1 oz (30 g)
½ teaspoon sake
½ teaspoon light soy sauce
2 fresh shrimp
2 fresh shiitake mushrooms
4 sprigs mitsuba or flat-leaf parsley
2 slices kamaboko fish cake (available at Japanese grocery stores), or other Asian fish cake

For the egg custard
1 egg
¾ cup (185 ml) dashi stock (see pages 6–7)
1 scant teaspoon mirin
1 scant teaspoon light soy sauce
Pinch of salt

1. Cut the chicken into bite-size pieces, and sprinkle with the sake and soy sauce. Peel the shrimp and devein (see page 56). Discard the stems of the shiitake mushrooms and cut the caps up into easy-to-eat pieces. Cut the mitsuba into 1¼ in (3 cm) pieces.

2. Make the egg custard. Beat the egg in a bowl, and add the other egg-custard ingredients. Push the mixture through a strainer.

3. Divide the chicken, shrimp, shiitake mushroom caps, kamaboko fish cake and mitsuba between 2 heatproof bowls or cups. Distribute the egg custard mixture evenly into the bowls or cups.

4. Cover the bowls or cups with cling film. Heat a steamer until the steam is rising, and put in the bowls or cups. Steam over high heat for 5 minutes. Remove the lid—if the custard looks pale and firm, turn the heat to low and steam for 15 minutes more. (If not, put the lid back on and steam over high heat for another minute.) They are done if the liquid runs clear when you poke the middle of a custard with a skewer. Take the containers out of the steamer and serve.

Seaweed Salad

Look for dried hijiki seaweed shoots, called *me-hijiki*, in your Japanese grocery store.

Sautéing the hijiki thoroughly eliminates any slight odor of seawater.

Serves 3 to 4 as a side dish

1 oz (30 g) dried hijiki seaweed shoots
½ piece thin-fried tofu (aburaage)
½ small carrot
1 teaspoon dark sesame oil
¾ cup (185 ml) dashi
1 tablespoon sake
1 tablespoon mirin
2 tablespoons dark soy sauce
1 tablespoon sugar

1. Rinse the hijiki seaweed, and soak in a generous amount of water until softened. Drain into a colander.

2. Put the aburaage in a colander and pour boiling water over it to remove the oil on the surface. Drain well. Cut into half lengthwise, and then cut into thin strips. Cut the carrot into thin strips too.

3. Heat the sesame oil in a pan, add the hijiki seaweed and stir-fry over medium heat. Add the carrot and aburaage and stir-fry some more. Add the dashi, sake, mirin, soy sauce and sugar. Cover with a small lid that fits right on top of the contents of the pan or a piece of kitchen parchment paper with a few holes poked in it. Simmer over low heat until the liquid has reduced to half its original volume.

1 block konnyaku, about 10 oz (300 g)
Vegetable oil, for stir-frying
½ red chili pepper, sliced into thin rounds
⅔ cup (160 ml) dashi stock (see pages 6–7)
1 tablespoon soy sauce
1½ tablespoons sake
1 tablespoon mirin
½ tablespoon sugar
1 handful bonito flakes (optional)

1. Cut the konnyaku into thumb-sized pieces. Bring a pan of water to a boil, add the konnyaku and boil for about 5 minutes. Drain into a colander.

2. Put the oil and red chili pepper in a pan over medium heat. When the pan is hot, add the konnyaku and stir-fry to dry out the pieces.

3. Combine the dashi, soy sauce, sake, mirin and sugar, and add the pan. When it comes to a boil turn the heat down to low, and simmer until there is just a little liquid left in the pan.

4. Add the bonito flakes and continue simmering until there is no moisture left in the pan.

Spicy Konnyaku with Bonito

The perfect accompaniment to plain rice.

A few strips kiriboshi daikon, about 1 oz (30 g)
½ small carrot
1 piece thin-fried tofu (aburaage)
1¼ cups (300 ml) dashi stock (see pages 6–7)
1½ tablespoons light soy sauce
2 tablespoons mirin
1 teaspoon sugar

1. Rinse the kiriboshi daikon briefly, and soak in cold water until softened. Drain and squeeze tightly. Cut the carrot into thin strips.

2. Put the aburaage in a colander and pour boiling water over it to remove the oil on the surface. Drain well. Cut into half lengthwise, and then cut into thin strips.

3. Put the dashi, soy sauce, mirin and sugar in a pan. Add the kiriboshi daikon and aburaage and bring to a boil over medium heat. When the liquid comes to a boil turn the heat down to low, and simmer while stirring occasionally until there is no liquid left in the pan.

Daikon Salad

Kiriboshi daikon is dehydrated daikon radish strips. You can find them at your Japanese market.

CHAPTER 4
Rice Dishes and Soups

This chapter includes colorful sushi for special occasions, as well as
everyday dishes centered on rice. The soups are ones you
will want to make again and again.

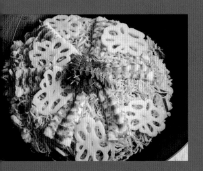

Sushi Rolls

Easy-to-eat and attractive, sushi is the perfect food for celebrations and par
The key to good sushi rolls is to roll them tightly so the fillings don't fall out
fillings that have a good balance of colors as well as flavors.

Makes 2 rolls

cups (500 g) cooked
  sushi rice
Japanese cucumber or
  ¼ English cucumber
mall bunch celery leaves
oz (250 g) cooked crab meat,
  drained of excess liquid
  and shredded or 8 pieces
  imitation crab, shredded

2 sheets nori seaweed,
  8 x 7 in (20 x 18 cm)
A little pickled ginger (gari)

Sweet Omelet
3 eggs
2 tablespoons dashi stock
  (see pages 6–7)
1–2 tablespoons sugar

**Simmered Shiitake
  Mushrooms**
2 dried shiitake mushrooms
¾ cup (185 ml) mushroom
  soaking liquid
1 tablespoon sugar
½ tablespoon mirin
1½ tablespoons soy sauce

Note: You can use
readymade eel in sauce
(kabayaki) instead of
crab. It's available in
Japanese grocery stores.

1. Make the sushi rice (see below).

2. Make the Sweet Omelet, following the instructions for Japanese Omelet on page 21. Cool and cut into ½ in (1 cm) strips.

3. Make the Simmered Shiitake Mushrooms. Soak the shiitake in hot water for 20 minutes to reconstitute, reserving the soaking liquid, and discard the stems. Put the shiitake with the rest of the simmering ingredients in a pan, and bring to a boil over medium heat. Turn the heat to low, and simmer until there is almost no liquid left in the pan. Cool, and slice the mushrooms into thin strips.

4. Cut the cucumber into strips. Blanch the celery leaves (see page 28 for how to blanch) and drain well.

5. Put a sheet of nori seaweed on a sushi mat, and spread out half the sushi rice on three quarters of the nori, starting from the edge closest to you. Make the rice a bit thinner for 1 in (2.5 cm) on the near edge.

6. Leaving some space on the near edge, put on the omelet, shiitake mushrooms, shredded crab and cucumber (see photo a). Holding down the fillings with your fingers, lift up the near edge of the sushi mat and start rolling (photo b). When the roll is rolled once, press and squeeze it with the sushi mat wrapped around it (photo c) and continue rolling. Press and squeeze again to tidy up the shape. Leave to rest for a few minutes.

7. With the seam side facing down, cut the roll into easy-to-eat pieces. Serve with a little pickled ginger on the side.

Sushi Rice

1½ cups (300 g) uncooked
  medium grain rice
1¼ cups (300 ml) water
4 in (10 cm) square piece
  dried kombu seaweed

For the sushi vinegar
4 tablespoons rice vinegar
1 tablespoon sugar
1 teaspoon salt

1. Rinse the rice and drain into a fine mesh sieve. Put the rice, water and kombu seaweed in a pot or rice cooker and cook the rice so that it's a bit firmer than regular cooked rice. (If cooking rice in a pot, see instructions on page 80.)

2. Combine the sushi vinegar ingredients and stir to dissolve the sugar and salt.

3. When the rice is cooked, remove the kombu seaweed (photo a) and empty out the rice into a bowl, wooden if possible. Add the sushi vinegar in one go, and mix the rice using a cut and fold motion while fanning it to cool it quickly (photo b).

Temari Sushi Balls

Cute, round sushi, called *temarizushi* in Japan, are perfect for festive occasions. In this recipe the raw fish toppings are marinated to give them deep, rich flavor.

Makes 10

- 4 oz (100 g) sashimi-grade sea bream, pre-sliced if available
- 1 teaspoon kombu tea powder
- 2 tablespoons sake
- 4 oz (100 g) sashimi-grade tuna, be pre-sliced if available
- 2 tablespoons soy sauce
- 1 tablespoon sake
- ½ tablespoon mirin
- 1 cup (250 g) prepared sushi rice (see page 71)

Garnishes
Finely shredded yuzu or lime zest
Fresh grated wasabi, or wasabi paste

1. Cut the sea bream into ¼ in (6 mm) diagonal slices. Combine the kombu tea and sake, and marinate the sea bream pieces in the mixture for about 5 minutes.

2. Cut the tuna into ¼ in (6 mm) diagonal slices. Combine the soy sauce, sake and mirin, and marinate the tuna pieces in the mixture for about 5 minutes.

3. Place a piece of sea bream on a square of cling film, and top with a small ball (about 2 teaspoons) of sushi rice. Twist the edges of the cling film to form an evenly round ball shape. Make 10 sea bream balls and 10 tuna balls in this way.

4. Remove the cling film from the formed balls and arrange on a plate. Top the sea bream balls with yuzu zest and the tuna balls with a little wasabi.

Inari Sushi

In this style of sushi, rice is stuffed into fried-tofu pockets that have been simmered in a savory-sweet sauce. Pack these into a large bento box to bring to potlucks or picnics.

Sesame seeds add texture to the rice and yuzu zest adds a fresh fragrance. If you don't have yuzu, try using lemon zest sparingly.

Makes 10

10 square or 5 rectangular pieces thin-fried tofu (aburaage)
3 teaspoons roasted white sesame seeds
A little finely chopped yuzu or lemon zest
1 cup (250 g) prepared sushi rice (see page 71)

For the simmering liquid
1¾ cups (425 ml) dashi stock (see pages 6–7)
2 tablespoons soy sauce
2 tablespoons mirin
3 tablespoons sugar

1. Put the aburaage pieces in a colander and pour boiling water over them to remove the surface oil. Roll a chopstick over them to push out the air. If using square pieces, cut them open at one end and open up to form bags. If using rectangular pieces, cut half so that you have two square bags.

2. Put the simmering liquid ingredients in a pan over medium heat and bring to a boil. Add the aburaage, turn the heat down to low and simmer until just a little liquid remains in the pan. Leave in the pan to cool and absorb more flavor.

3. Add the sesame seeds and yuzu zest to the sushi rice and mix. Divide into 10 portions, and form into oval balls.

4. Drain the aburaage lightly, and stuff with the rice balls.

73

Chirashi Sushi Bowl

Sometimes called "scattered sushi," this is sushi rice with various colorful toppings. If you serve a big plate of chirashi sushi with splashes of red, yellow and green, your dinner table will become instantly festive. It does take some time to prep the toppings, but the results are well worth it.

Serves 4

3 medium to large fresh shrimp
2 cups (500 g) prepared sushi rice
  (see page 71)
4 Simmered Shiitake Mushrooms
  (see page 71)
A few sansho pepper or shiso
  leaves, or blanched snow peas

Lotus Root in Vinegar Sauce
(optional)
1 piece lotus root, 2 in (5 cm) thick
Water, for soaking, with a little
  vinegar added
3 tablespoons rice vinegar
1½ tablespoons sugar
A little salt
3 tablespoons water

Simmered Carrot
½ small carrot
½ cup (125 ml) dashi stock
  (see pages 6–7)
2 teaspoons light soy sauce
2½ teaspoons mirin
A little salt

Shredded Egg Crepes
2 eggs
A little salt
Oil, for cooking

1. Peel the shrimp, devein them (see page 56) and put on bamboo skewers to keep them straight while they cook. Boil briefly in salted water. Cool, then cut into the belly side to butterfly them.

2. Make the Lotus Root in Vinegar Sauce, if using. Peel and slice the lotus root very thinly. If you like you can cut the slices into flower shapes as shown in the photo opposite. Soak the slices in water with a little vinegar added. Bring a small pan of water to a boil. Remove the slices from the vinegared water, put them in the small pan of boiling water, and boil for 3 minutes. Drain. Combine the rice vinegar, sugar, salt and water, and marinate the lotus root slices in it.

3. Make the Simmered Carrot. Shred the carrot. Put all the other Simmered Carrot ingredients in a pan over medium heat and bring to a boil. Add the carrot and cook for 1 minute. Turn off the heat, let cool, and drain.

4. Make the Shredded Egg Crepes. Beat the eggs and add the salt. Heat a frying pan and spread with vegetable oil, or white sesame oil if you have it. Spread a thin layer of the beaten egg in the frying pan. When the surface of the egg is dry, quickly flip the egg over, then take it out of the pan to cool. Repeat until all the beaten egg is used up. Shred the crepes into long, thin strips.

5. Put the sushi rice in a bowl, add the Simmered Shiitake Mushrooms and the Simmered Carrot, and mix.

6. Transfer the rice to a serving plate and top with the shredded egg crepe, shrimp and lotus root in that order. Garnish with sansho pepper leaves or shiso leaves, or snow peas.

VARIATION

Smoked Mackerel and Cucumber Chirashi Sushi Bowl

A refreshing light sushi, perfect for summer.

Serves 2

2 oz (60 g) smoked mackerel
  or trout
½ tablespoon rice vinegar
1 Japanese cucumber or
  ½ English cucumber, deseeded

1 small piece young ginger,
  or 1 myoga bud
1 cup (250 g) prepared sushi rice
  (see page 71)

1. Sprinkle the fish with the vinegar and leave for 5 minutes. Shred with your hands into pieces.

2. Slice the cucumber into thin rounds, sprinkle with salt and rub it in. Leave for 10 minutes, and squeeze out tightly. Chop up the ginger finely.

3. Add the fish, cucumber and ginger to the rice and mix gently.

Mixed Rice Bowls

Rice cooked with a variety of umami-rich ingredients like chicken and vegetables is so tasty you won't be able to resist a second helping!

Serves 3 to 4

1 boneless chicken thigh, about 4 oz (100g)
Sake, for sprinkling
¼ burdock root (optional)
½ carrot (use a whole carrot if you can't
   get hold of burdock root)
2 fresh shiitake mushrooms
½ piece thin-fried tofu (aburaage)
1¼ cups (250 g) uncooked rice
1 cup (250 ml) dashi stock (see pages 6–7)
1 tablespoon light soy sauce
2 teaspoons mirin

1. Dice the chicken and sprinkle it with a little sake.

2. If using the burdock root, shave it with a knife or a vegetable peeler into thin strips (see page 28), and soak in a bowl of water. Drain into a colander. Cut the carrot into matchsticks. Remove and discard the stems from the shiitake and slice the caps thinly.

3. Put the aburaage in a colander and pour boiling water over it to remove the oil on the surface. Drain well. Cut into half lengthwise, and then cut into thin strips.

4. Rinse the rice and drain (see page 80). Put all the ingredients into a pot or rice cooker, and cook until the rice is done. Roughly stir the rice before serving.

Chicken and Egg Rice Bowl

The key to the dish is the creamy, soft-set egg.

Serves 2

2 boneless chicken thighs, about 8 oz (250 g) total
2 green onions (scallions)
3 beaten eggs
2 bowls warm cooked rice

Simmering liquid
⅔ cup (160 ml) dashi stock (see pages 6–7)
1 tablespoon light soy sauce
2 tablespoons mirin

1. Cut the chicken into diagonal bite-size pieces. Slice the green onions diagonally.

2. Put the simmering liquid ingredients into a pan over medium heat. When it comes to a boil add the chicken. When the chicken is just about cooked through, add the green onion. Pour in the beaten eggs. When they are soft-set, turn off the heat, cover with a lid and rest for 30 seconds.

3. Top each bowl of rice with the chicken-and-egg mixture, while shaking the pan around to loosen the contents.

Beef Rice Bowl

Savory and sweet, this is the king of rice bowls.

Serves 2

8 oz (250 g) thinly sliced beef
½ medium onion
Small piece ginger, peeled
2 bowls warm cooked rice
Shredded red ginger (beni shoga), for garnish

Simmering liquid
3 tablespoons soy sauce
2 tablespoons sake
2 tablespoons mirin
2 tablespoons raw sugar
¾ cup (185 ml) water

1. Cut the beef into bite-size pieces. Slice the onion thinly. Finely shred the ginger.

2. Put the simmering liquid ingredients in a pan over medium heat. When it comes to a boil add the onion and ginger, and cook until the onion has wilted. Add the beef and stir around to separate the pieces. Skim off any scum.

3. When the beef is cooked through, turn the heat to high and mix the contents of the pan well to make sure everything is coated with the sauce. Place equal portions of beef on the two bowls of rice, and garnish with the shredded red ginger.

Pork and Vegetable Soup

Serves 2

4 oz (100 g) sliced pork shoulder
¼ carrot
5 oz (125 g) daikon radish, peeled
2 thin slices fresh lotus root, peeled (optional)
1 fresh shiitake mushroom
½ tablespoon dark sesame oil
1½ cups (375 ml) dashi stock (see pages 6–7)
1½ tablespoons miso paste
Chopped green onion (scallion), for garnish

1. Cut the pork into bite-size pieces. Slice the carrot and daikon thinly, then cut each slice into quarters. Quarter the lotus root slices, if using. Cut off and discard the stem of the shiitake and slice the cap thinly.

2. Heat the sesame oil in a frying pan, add the pork and stir-fry. When the meat changes color add the carrot, lotus root (if using), daikon radish and shiitake and stir-fry. When everything is coated with the oil, add the dashi stock.

3. Bring to a boil, skim off the scum, and simmer for 20 minutes.

4. When the vegetables are tender, dissolve the miso in a little of the broth and add to the pan.

5. Ladle into soup bowls, and top with some chopped green onion.

Creamy Turnip Soup

Serves 2

1 turnip, about 5 oz (125 g)
1¼ cups (300 ml) dashi stock (see pages 6–7)
1½ tablespoons white miso paste
Finely sliced green onion (scallion), for garnish
Turnip leaf, for garnish

1. Peel the turnip and slice thinly.

2. Put the dashi stock and the turnip in a pan over medium heat. Bring to a boil and turn the heat to low. Cool slightly, put the contents of the pan into a blender, and blend until you have a smooth soup.

3. Pour the soup back into the pan. Dissolve the miso with a little of the soup, and add to the pan. Heat the soup over medium heat. Serve topped with green onion and a little turnip leaf.

Fish Cake Soup

1 fresh sardine, about 5 oz (125 g)
Small piece peeled ginger
2 teaspoons miso paste
1 tablespoon flour
Pinch sansho pepper, or cayenne pepper
1¼ cup (300 ml) kombu dashi stock (see pages 6–7)
1 large Napa cabbage leaf, roughly chopped
1 tablespoon miso paste
Sansho pepper, or cayenne pepper, for garnish

1 Remove the head of the sardine and clean, removing any bones (see page 56). Rinse under running water and pat dry. Remove the skin and the spine. Chop the fish up roughly. Chop the ginger roughly. Put the sardine and ginger plus the 2 teaspoons of miso, the flour and the pinch of sansho pepper into a food processor and mix.

2 Bring the kombu dashi to a boil in a pan. Form the fish mixture into bite-size balls, and drop into the dashi. Bring the pan back to a boil and skim off the scum. Add the Napa cabbage leaf and simmer until tender.

3 Dissolve the 1 tablespoon of miso in a little of the broth and add to the pan. Serve in bowls sprinkled with a little sansho or cayenne pepper.

Root Vegetable Miso Soup

A few strips thin-fried tofu (aburaage)
A few strips konnyaku (optional) about 2 oz (50 g)
Small piece burdock root, or turnip, about 1 oz (30 g)
¼ carrot, cut into matchsticks
Small piece taro root, about 2 oz (50 g), or ¼ parsnip
½ block firm tofu
½ tablespoon dark sesame oil
1¾ cups (425 ml) dashi stock (see pages 6–7)
2 teaspoons light soy sauce
1 tablespoon sake
¼ teaspoon salt

1 Put the aburaage in a colander, and pour boiling water over it to remove the surface oil. Drain and cut into strips. Cut the konnyaku, if using, into small pieces and boil briefly. Scrape the skin off the burdock root if using (see page 28), or peel the turnip. Cut the burdock root or turnip into thin slices. Soak the slices briefly in water, and drain. Peel the taro root or parsnip and cut into 3 to 4 pieces. Cut the tofu into small cubes.

2 Heat the dark sesame oil in a pan. Add all the ingredients from Step 1 to the pan and stir-fry. Add the dashi, light soy sauce, sake and salt to the pan, and simmer for about 10 minutes.

Everyday Techniques

Reconstituting shiitake

You can reconstitute dried shiitake mushrooms in hot water in 20 minutes, but they will retain more flavor if reconstituted slowly. To do so, cover with cold water and soak for 5 hours in the refrigerator. You can soak a whole bag of shiitake at once, wring them out, and freeze them in a single layer on a tray. Put the frozen mushrooms in freezer bags.

Draining tofu

Wrap the tofu in paper towels and place in a shallow tray. Put another tray on top and weigh it down. Discard the water that comes out of the tofu several times.

Roasting sesame seeds and grinding

Put the sesame seeds in a small frying pan. Hold the pan a little away from the heat (if using gas) and shake until roasted. Put the roasted seeds in a grinding bowl with a moistened and wrung out kitchen towel underneath to hold it in place. Grind with a pestle until completely crushed.

Making a drop lid

A "drop lid" goes inside a pan, directly on top of the contents, to keep everything immersed in the liquid so that it cooks evenly. Take a square piece of kitchen parchment paper about the same circumference as your pan. Fold over once, then fold again so that you have a small square. Cut the square in an arc from the corner of one of the open sides to the other. Then fold the paper over once into a triangle and cut off the point (top photo). Open up (bottom photo), and you have a drop lid! To simmer while skimming off scum, use a crumpled-up piece of aluminum foil as a drop lid. Use microwave-safe paper towels as the drop lid when you want to cook down the liquid in the pan—don't worry, they won't dissolve. If you use a drop lid made of kitchen parchment paper, you can simmer while keeping the cooking liquid from cooking off completely.

How to cook rice

1 Put the uncooked rice in a bowl, and pour in water.

2 Mix briefly, then drain off the water.

3 Put 1 in (2.5 cm) of water into the bottom of the bowl with the rice. Stir the rice about 10 times with your hands, rinse briefly with more water, and drain. Repeat 3–4 times.

4 Add water to the rice to cover, and soak for 30 minutes to an hour.

5 Drain into a fine mesh sieve.

6 Put the rice into a pot or rice cooker, and add water. Use an equal volume water and rice, i.e., 1 cup of water for 1 cup of rice. If you want firm rice, use about 5–10% less water.

7 Put a lid on the pot and place over high heat. When the water boils, turn the heat to low and cook for 12 minutes. Turn off the heat and leave the pot to steam with residual heat for 10 minutes.

8 Open the pot and stir the rice with a moistened paddle.

9 Stir the rice completely from the bottom to aerate it all around.

CHAPTER 5

Modern Twists on Classic Dishes

For a change of pace, this chapter takes classic Japanese recipes and gives them an international flavor. They are sure to become firm favorites!

Japanese-style Beef Stew

This recipe builds on a French classic with its rich flavors of red wine, and adds a Japanese twist with miso, dashi stock and zingy peppercorns. It's a dish worthy of very special occasions.

Serves 2

1 in (2.5 cm) piece celery stalk
8 broccolini florets
1 baby leek or fat green onion
4 fresh shiitake mushrooms
10 oz (300 g) boneless beef rib
Salt and pepper
Oil, for cooking
½ cup (125 ml) red wine
½ tablespoon green peppercorns in brine
2 tablespoons ginger juice (grate fresh ginger and
    squeeze it to extract the juice)
2 tablespoons cornstarch
2 tablespoons water

For the simmering liquid
2 in (5 cm) square piece dried kombu seaweed
¾ cup (185 ml) sake
2½ cups (625 ml) water

The flavorings
2 tablespoons red miso paste
1 tablespoon white miso paste
1 tablespoon dark soy sauce
4 tablespoons honey

1 Remove the tough outer fibers from the celery and chop up roughly. Boil the broccolini briefly in salted water. Cut into 1¼ in (3 cm) long pieces and drain well. Cut the leek into 1¼ in (3 cm) long pieces, and sauté in a frying pan with a little oil added, rolling the pieces around until lightly browned. Cut the stems off the shiitake mushrooms and discard. Slice the shiitake caps.

2 Cut the beef into 1½ in (4 cm) cubes and season with salt and pepper. Heat some oil in a pan over medium high heat, and brown the beef cubes well. Take the beef out of the pan, and put in the celery. Sauté until it is limp.

3 Add the red wine to the pan and simmer over medium heat for 1 to 2 minutes. Put the beef back in, plus the Simmering Liquid ingredients. Bring to a boil, take out the kombu seaweed, and turn the heat down to a low simmer. Simmer for about 2 hours, removing any scum that rises to the surface.

4 Add the flavorings and the peppercorns in that order. Continue simmering until the liquid in the pan is reduced to about half its original volume.

5 Add the ginger juice and mix in. Dissolve the cornstarch in the 2 tablespoons of water, and add to the pan. Simmer while stirring until the sauce has thickened. Add the leek and shiitake mushrooms from Step 1, and continue simmering until they are cooked through. Serve garnished with the broccolini.

Brown the surface of the beef well to lock in the flavor (photo a). Don't forget to take out the kombu seaweed once the simmering liquid comes to a boil (photo b).

Pan-fried Spare Ribs with Sesame Sauce

The assertive flavors of the thick sauce made from sesame and miso are a good match for the slowly cooked pork.

Serves 2 to 3

10 oz (300 g) pork spare ribs
Salt, for sprinkling
1 tablespoon vegetable oil
1 sprig watercress, to garnish

For the sesame sauce
2 tablespoons tahini, or sesame paste
2 teaspoons miso paste
1½ tablespoons dark soy sauce
1 tablespoon sake
1 tablespoon mirin
1 tablespoon vegetable oil (see Note)

Note: Light sesame oil made from unroasted white sesame seeds is recommended if you can find it.

Making several small cuts into the meat will help it cook faster.

Wipe out the fat that is exuded from the spare ribs so that they don't become greasy.

The spare ribs can burn once the sauce is added, so turn the heat down and watch the pan as you turn the ribs in the sauce to coat.

1 Make several small cuts in each spare rib on both sides. Sprinkle lightly with salt.

2 Combine the sesame sauce ingredients in a bowl and mix well.

3 Heat the vegetable oil in a frying pan. Add the prepped spare ribs and brown over medium heat, turning several times. Wipe out any fat that comes out of them using paper towels.

4 Add the sauce from Step 2 to the frying pan, and continue cooking over low heat. When the ribs are cooked through, transfer to a serving plate and garnish with the watercress.

Pasta with Tuna and Capers

Not only can this dish be made with stock pantry items, it's also very easy to put together. Grated Parmesan cheese, soy sauce and sour capers make a surprisingly good match!

Serves 2

5 oz (125 g) uncooked spaghetti
1 can tuna in oil
4 tablespoons grated Parmesan
  cheese
1 teaspoon capers in brine
1½ teaspoons soy sauce
1 tablespoon olive oil
Salt and black pepper, to taste
Crumbled nori seaweed, for garnish

1 Bring a pot of salted water to a boil, and cook the spaghetti until al dente. Reserve a little of the cooking water.

2 Drain the oil from the canned tuna and put into a large bowl. Flake the tuna and add the cheese, capers, soy sauce and olive oil.

3 Add the spaghetti plus 1 or 2 tablespoons of the cooking water to the bowl. Mix well.

4 Sprinkle with salt and black pepper, to taste. Transfer to serving plates and sprinkle with some crumbled nori seaweed.

Lemony Sea Bream Salad

This salad features fresh sea bream marinated in lemon. If you can't get fresh sashimi-grade sea bream, you can simply omit it, make the marinade, and pour it over the vegetables as a dressing—the salad will still taste really good!

After putting the sea bream in the marinade, turn it once and then leave for 10 minutes. The surface of the fish will "cook," and the contrast with the still-uncooked inside of the fish will be fantastic!

Serves 2

5 oz (125 g) sashimi-
  grade sea bream
Salt, for sprinkling
Grated lemon zest,
  for garnish

For the marinade
½ tablespoon white miso paste
½ tablespoon light soy sauce
1 tablespoon lemon juice
1 tablespoon olive oil

Accompaniments
Baby leaf salad
3 radishes

1. Slice the sea bream into thin slices about a tenth of an inch (3 mm) thick. Sprinkle lightly with salt.

2. Put the marinade ingredients in a bowl and mix well to combine. Transfer to a shallow tray. Put in the sliced sea bream in a single layer, and marinate for about 10 minutes.

3. Arrange some baby leaf salad and thinly sliced radishes in two bowls, and top with the marinated sea bream. Pour the remaining marinade on top, and scatter with a little lemon zest.

Smoked Fish and Potato Salad

Pan-fried Scallops with Wasabi

2 oz (50 g) smoked fish (see Note)
1 small or ¼ regular cucumber
10 green shiso leaves or basil leaves
2 medium potatoes
½ tablespoon white wine vinegar or rice vinegar
4 tablespoons mayonnaise
Salt and pepper, to taste

Note: In Japan this recipe is often made with salted mackerel (shio saba) which can be found at Japanese grocery stores. This recipe works with any kind of smoked fish—you don't need to grill it before using.

1 (If using salted mackerel, grill until lightly browned, then remove the bones and skin.) Shred the fish. Slice the cucumber (deseed first if the seeds are large) and sprinkle with salt. Leave for 5 minutes, the squeeze tightly to eliminate excess moisture. Finely shred the shiso or basil leaves, soak briefly in a bowl of cold water, and drain well.

2 Boil the potatoes in salted water until tender. Peel the potatoes while they're still hot, and mash roughly. Sprinkle with the vinegar and mix briefly.

3 Add all the ingredients to the potatoes and mix. Taste, and adjust the seasoning with salt and pepper.

1 tablespoon light sesame oil or vegetable oil
4–5 fresh scallops
½ Belgian endive or chicory
¼ small lime, to garnish

For the sauce
A little wasabi paste (see Note), or English mustard
Juice of 1 small lime
1 teaspoon light soy sauce
1 teaspoon rice vinegar

Note: If you can find wasabi zuke, a Japanese condiment where the leaves and stems of the wasabi plant are preserved in sake lees, use 1 tablespoon of this instead of the wasabi paste or English mustard.

1 Heat the oil in a frying pan, add the scallops, and brown quickly on both sides over medium high heat. Take the scallops out and cut each into quarters.

2 Cut the leaves of the endive into ½ in (1 cm) wide pieces.

3 Combine the sauce ingredients in a bowl, and add the scallops and endive. Mix to coat. Arrange on a serving plate with the lime quarter.

Tuna and Mozzarella Side Salad

Squid and Avocado with Miso Dressing

Serves 2

oz (100 g) sashimi-grade raw tuna
oz (50 g) mozzarella cheese
ablespoon nori paste (see Note)
little wasabi paste, or English mustard

te: Nori paste (nori no tsukudani) is a condiment made with nori
aweed, soy sauce, sugar and other flavors. It is sold in jars and
ailable at Japanese grocery stores. If you cannot find it, substitute
ri flakes mixed with a bit of soy sauce and mirin.

Cut the tuna and mozzarella cheese into ¾ in (2 cm) cubes.

Put the tuna and mozzarella into a bowl, add the nori paste and mix well.

Serve topped with a little wasabi paste.

Serves 2

1 green onion (scallion)
½ avocado
A little lemon juice
4 oz (100 g) fresh sashimi-grade squid

For the sauce
2 tablespoons white miso paste
2 tablespoons rice vinegar
2 tablespoons raw sugar
A little Japanese mustard, or English mustard

1 Cut the roots and tip off the green onion. Boil briefly until crisp-tender, drain well and cut into 1½ in (4 cm) long pieces.

2 Cut the avocado into bite-size pieces. Sprinkle with lemon juice to prevent it from discoloring.

3 Prepare the squid if necessary, following the instructions on page 56. Cut into bite-size pieces.

4 Combine the sauce ingredients in a bowl and mix well. Add the green onions, avocado and squid, and mix to coat everything with the sauce.

Chicken and Potato Casserole

This is a an easy dish that you can just put in the oven and forget about. Since it is baked with the lid on, be sure to blanch the chicken beforehand to prevent it from getting too gamy.

Serves 2

2 boneless chicken thighs, about
  8 oz (250 g) total
Salt, for sprinkling
2 medium potatoes, about 8 oz
  (250 g)
1¼ cups (300 ml) dashi
1 tablespoon dark soy sauce
1 tablespoon sake
1½ tablespoons sugar

1 Trim the chicken thighs (see page 13) and cut into 8 pieces. Sprinkle lightly with salt. Bring a pot of water to a boil, and blanch the chicken (see page 41 for how to blanch). Drain in a colander.

2 Peel the potatoes, cut into bite-size pieces and put into a bowl of cold water for a few minutes. Drain.

3 Put the chicken, potatoes and all the other ingredients into an ovenproof heavy pot, and heat over medium heat. Turn the heat off just before the liquid comes to a full boil, turn the heat down to low and skim off any scum.

4 Cover the pot with a lid, and bake in a preheated oven at 320°F (160°C) for an hour.

Pork-wrapped Tempura

Vegetables wrapped in thinly sliced pork and paper-thin kombu seaweed are deep-fried, tempura style. The tomato and leek inside are a soft and juicy contrast to the crispy shell.

Serves 2

long leek
2 thin slices pork loin
salt, for sprinkling
cherry tomatoes
2 pieces oboro kombu seaweed
(see Note), or nori seaweed
oil, for deep-frying

For the batter
5 tablespoons flour
1 beaten egg
½ cup (125 ml) water

1 Cut the leek into 6 pieces, each about 1½ in (4 cm) long. Spread out the pork slices and sprinkle with salt.

2 Wrap a piece of leek in 6 of the pork slices and a cherry tomato in the other 6 slices. Wrap each of the 12 pork rolls with oboro kombu.

3 Mix together the batter ingredients.

4 Heat some oil in a pan or deep frying pan to 340°F (170°C). Dip the rolls into the batter, and put into the hot oil. Turn the rolls when the surface has firmed up, and fry until crispy. Drain well before serving.

Note: Oboro kombu is kombu seaweed that has been shaved into paper-thin pieces. It is available at Japanese grocery stores. If you cannot find it, use nori seaweed instead.

Chicken Meatball Hot Pot

Warming hot pots are great when the weather is cold. How about giving this unusual soy-milk based hot pot a try?

Serves 2

1 burdock root or
  parsnip
1 bunch water celery
  (see Note)

For the meatballs
4 oz (100 g) fresh medium whole shrimp
4 oz (100 g) ground chicken
⅔ teaspoon ginger juice (grate ginger
  and squeeze to extract the juice)
½ beaten egg
1 teaspoon sake
A little salt

For the broth
4 cups (1 L) kombu dashi stock
½ cup (125 ml) light soy sauce
½ cup (125 ml) mirin
½ cup (125 ml) sake
¼–½ cup (65–125 ml)
  unsweetened soy milk

Note: Water celery, also called dropwort, Chinese celery or Japanese celery is a crisp green leafy vegetable. You can find it at general Asian grocery stores. Mizuna greens or watercress are good substitutes.

1 Scrub the skin off the burdock root, if using, with a stiff vegetable brush or a wad of crumpled up aluminum foil, and rinse. Peel the parsnip, if using. Cut the burdock or parsnip into long, thin slices using a vegetable peeler. Cut the roots off the water celery, then cut in half.

2 Make the meatballs. Peel the shrimp, take off the heads and tails, and remove the intestines (see page 56). Chop up roughly. Put all the meatball ingredients into a bowl, and mix well until the chicken is sticky. Form into bite-size balls.

3 Put all the broth ingredients except for the soy milk into an earthenware pot or a heavy pan, and heat over medium heat. When it comes to a boil, add the meatballs, and simmer over medium-low heat for 5–6 minutes. When the meatballs are cooked through, add the soy milk, burdock root and water celery. Lower the heat, and simmer for 1-2 minutes, taking care not to let it come to a full boil.

To finish your hot pot meal...

Pork Broth Ramen

If there is any broth left over from your Chicken Meatball Hot Pot (above), put it in a pan with a few goji berries, a small piece of ginger sliced thinly and one crushed garlic clove, and bring to a boil. Boil some Chinese egg noodles separately until they are still firm, add them to the broth, and bring back to a boil. Serve in bowls topped with a little sesame chili oil. This type of dish, which consists of some kind of carbohydrate (here it's noodles, but it can be rice, mochi cakes, and so on), is called the *shime* in Japan, and is usually served as the final course of a meal. This delicious shime is really easy to eat, even if you're full!

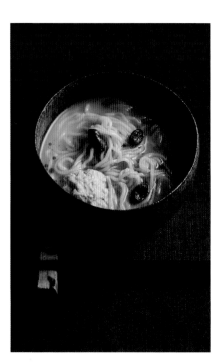

Tomato and Olive Rice

his delicious rice dish has a Mediterranean flavor.

Serves 2

ripe, sweet tomatoes
4 cups (250 g) uncooked Japanese rice
in (5cm) square piece kombu seaweed
4 cups (300 ml) water
5 pitted black olives, torn into 2–3 pieces each
cup (50 g) chirimenjako (see Note), or dried, salted whitebait
tablespoons olive oil

ote: Chirimenjako are tiny salted and semi-dried sardines, available
Japanese grocery stores, or substitute with dried, salted whitebait.
nother substitute is chopped walnuts, which have a similar texture.

1. Bring a pot of water to a boil. Make a shallow crisscross cut on the bottom of each tomato, and quickly dunk into the boiling water. Take out and peel off the skin. Cut each tomato into 4 wedges.

2. Rinse the rice several times under running water, and drain into a fine mesh sieve or colander. Put the rice, kombu seaweed, water, tomatoes and olives into a pot or a rice cooker, and cook the rice (see page 80 for how to cook rice in a pot). The rice grains should still be on the firm side when cooked.

3. Mix the chirimenjako with the olive oil.

4. Mix the cooked rice using a cut-and-fold motion, put into serving bowls and top with the chirimenjako.

Clam and Vegetable Soup

lams are highly nutritious and also packed with umami.

Serves 2

oz (200 g) asari or Manila clams
carrot
medium potato
celery stalk
in (10 cm) square piece dried kombu seaweed
tablespoons sake
½ cups (375 ml) water
tablespoons canned soy beans, or lima beans
oy sauce, to taste
alt and pepper, to taste
hopped parsley, for garnish

1. Clean the clams following the instructions on page 56.

2. Dice the carrot and potato. Remove the tough outer fibers from the celery, and dice.

3. Put the clams, kombu seaweed, sake and water in a pot over medium heat. Bring to a boil, take out the kombu seaweed, and skim off any scum. Add the carrot, potato, celery and soy beans.

4. When the clams have opened up and the vegetables are cooked, add the soy sauce, salt and pepper while tasting the broth. Serve with some parsley scattered on top.

"Books to Span the East and West"

Tuttle Publishing was founded in 1832 in the small New England town of Rutland, Vermont [USA]. Our core values remain as strong today as they were then—to publish best-in-class books which bring people together one page at a time. In 1948, we established a publishing outpost in Japan—and Tuttle is now a leader in publishing English-language books about the arts, languages and cultures of Asia. The world has become a much smaller place today and Asia's economic and cultural influence has grown. Yet the need for meaningful dialogue and information about this diverse region has never been greater. Over the past seven decades, Tuttle has published thousands of books on subjects ranging from martial arts and paper crafts to language learning and literature—and our talented authors, illustrators, designers and photographers have won many prestigious awards. We welcome you to explore the wealth of information available on Asia at **www.tuttlepublishing.com**.

Published by Tuttle Publishing, an imprint of Periplus Editions (HK) Ltd.

www.tuttlepublishing.com

CHANTO OBOETAI WASHOKU
Copyright ©Asako Yoshida 2018
All rights reserved.
English translation rights arranged with SHUWA SYSTEM CO., LTD., through Japan UNI Agency, Tokyo

English translation by Makiko Itoh. English translation copyright ©2020 Periplus Editions (HK) Ltd.

ISBN 978-4-8053-1581-1

First edition
26 25 24 23   8 7 6 5 4 3 2

Printed in China   2308EP

TUTTLE PUBLISHING® is a registered trademark of Tuttle Publishing, a division of Periplus Editions (HK) Ltd.

Distributed by

North America, Latin America & Europe
Tuttle Publishing
364 Innovation Drive
North Clarendon, VT 05759-9436 U.S.A.
Tel: 1 (802) 773-8930
Fax: 1 (802) 773-6993
info@tuttlepublishing.com
www.tuttlepublishing.com

Japan
Tuttle Publishing
Yaekari Building, 3rd Floor, 5-4-12 Osaki
Shinagawa-ku, Tokyo 141 0032
Tel: (81) 3 5437-0171
Fax: (81) 3 5437-0755
sales@tuttle.co.jp
www.tuttle.co.jp

Asia Pacific
Berkeley Books Pte Ltd
3 Kallang Sector #04-01
Singapore 349278
Tel: (65) 6741 2178
Fax: (65) 6741 2179
inquiries@periplus.com.sg
www.tuttlepublishing.com